The Complexities of Equity

The Complexities of Equity

Navigating Shades of Gray in Schools and Organizations

Latish C. Reed

Learn more about bringing Dr. Reed to your school or organization at reedlead.com.

FOR INFORMATION:

Corwin
A SAGE Company
2455 Teller Road
Thousand Oaks, California 91320
(800) 233-9936
www.corwin.com

SAGE Publications Ltd.
1 Oliver's Yard
55 City Road
London EC1Y 1SP
United Kingdom

SAGE Publications India Pvt. Ltd.
Unit No 323-333, Third Floor, F-Block
International Trade Tower Nehru Place
New Delhi 110 019
India

SAGE Publications Asia-Pacific Pte. Ltd.
18 Cross Street #10-10/11/12
China Square Central
Singapore 048423

Vice President and Editorial Director: Monica Eckman
Acquisitions Editor: Megan Bedell
Content Development Manager: Lucas Schleicher
Senior Editorial Assistant: Natalie Delpino
Project Editor: Amy Schroller
Copy Editor: Lynne Curry
Typesetter: C&M Digitals (P) Ltd.
Cover Designer: Candice Harman
Marketing Manager: Melissa Duclos

Printed and bound by CPI Group (UK) Ltd, Croydon, CR0 4YY

Library of Congress Cataloging-in-Publication Data

Names: Reed, Latish C., author.

Title: The complexities of equity : navigating shades of gray in schools and organizations / Latish C. Reed.

Description: Thousand Oaks, California : Corwin, [2025] | Includes bibliographical references and index.

Identifiers: LCCN 2024051626 | ISBN 9781071940266 (paperback) | ISBN 9781071940273 (epub) | ISBN 9781071940280 (epub) | ISBN 9781071940297 (pdf)

Subjects: LCSH: Educational equalization. | Educational change. | Youth with social disabilities—Education. | Diversity in the workplace.

Classification: LCC LC213 .R434 2025 | DDC 379.2/6—dc23/eng/20250206
LC record available at https://lccn.loc.gov/2024051626

This book is printed on acid-free paper.

25 26 27 28 29 10 9 8 7 6 5 4 3 2 1

Contents

Website Contents

For downloadable versions of the forms above, please visit the companion website at **https://companion.corwin.com/courses/ComplexitiesofEquity**

Preface

Navigating Shifting Election Outcomes and Their Impact

November 4, 2008—President Barack H. Obama was elected.

November 6, 2012—President Barack H. Obama was reelected.

November 8, 2016—President Donald J. Trump was elected.

November 3, 2020—President Joseph R. Biden was elected.

November 5, 2024—President Donald J. Trump was reelected.

As a layperson, I have always been fascinated by politics. My high school social studies teacher, Sonja Ivanovich, inspired me to become a middle school social studies teacher. In her class, she required that we analyze current events and political implications in newspaper and Public Broadcasting Service (PBS) television content. I learned that shifts in political power can have significant social, economic, cultural, legal, judicial, and environmental impacts in the United States and worldwide. The sixteen-year span of the five election cycles outlined above illustrates a ping-pong in political ideologies that impacts efforts to curate more equity in the US. Free and fair elections are one of the cornerstones of our democracy. Fortunately, or unfortunately, election results determine how equitable actions can be enacted or whether they can be enacted at all. Large-scale policy shifts impact equitable outcomes. These five election cycles have unearthed polarizing differences within the electorate that will continue to impact equity work and how it is advocated for in the future. These swings provide the backdrop for *The Complexities of Equity: Navigating Shades of Gray in Schools and Other Organizations*.

When Barack Obama was elected the first African American president, it seemed to be a strong signal that the US was ready to turn the page on its history marred by its enslavement of Black Americans. Some, like David Schorr of National Public Radio, claimed this symbolized a postracial society

(Schorr, 2008). At the time, he wrote, "The post-racial era, as embodied by Obama, is the era where civil rights veterans of the past century are consigned to history and Americans begin to make race-free judgments on who should lead them." Obama's historical election showed that white Americans would vote for and elect a Black man—a clear sign of racism's death or so he suggested.

However, following Obama's election, a bold new conservative faction of the Republican Party emerged that opposed the economic stimulus package following the 2008 financial recession. Its opposition was parallel to a rise in racialized rhetoric against Obama's presidency (Willer, Feinberg, & Wetts, 2016). The Tea Party moved from a grassroots protest group to an organization capable of winning seats in Congress within a year and a half of its inception. Willer et al. (2016) explain how Obama's election seemed to garner attention to the perceived social footing lost by white America because of the election of a Black man. Michael Dimock (2017) of the Pew Institute provided some evidence to substantiate that assertion. According to his prediction, "In less than 40 years, the U.S. will not have a single racial or ethnic majority group." Forecasts like this seemed to stoke fears among white voters, building a steady opposition to the changing tide in the US.

Throughout the Obama years, dissatisfaction among Tea Party members and their supporters grew because Obama's leadership provided equitable initiatives in several areas. The Tea Party and its supporters began to feel that their values were being threatened and their resources were being redistributed, diminishing their status. For example, the Affordable Healthcare Act (ACA) (Obamacare) became one of the most contentious but equitable accomplishments of his presidency. The ACA covered millions of previously uninsured Americans (Kors, 2012). Citizens could no longer be denied or overcharged for coverage due to preexisting conditions. According to the US Department of Health and Human Services (n.d.), the ACA also expanded Medicaid, increasing access for more low-income citizens. Obama also took on gender equality issues by signing the Lilly Ledbetter Fair Pay Act of 2009 (Equal Pay Act, 2009), allowing individuals to combat gender wage discrimination.

Furthermore, the Obama administration confronted discrimination against LGBTQIA+ communities. He signed the repeal of the "Don't Ask, Don't Tell" military edict that forced individuals to conceal their sexual orientation and identity, allowing them to serve openly in the military (Gay Stolberg, 2010). The Obama administration also provided guidance and support for best practices in schools to serve the needs of LGBTQIA+ students (Horsley, 2016). Obama's administration interpreted Title IX's sense of nondiscrimination to mean protection for trans students. Yet, advancing equitable causes like these stoked a new wave of discontent among many Americans. This profound sense of loss made way for what was to come.

In the summer of 2015, Donald J. Trump, a businessman and reality TV personality, announced his candidacy for the 2016 presidential election at Trump Tower, a building he owned and named after himself. In his speech announcing his candidacy, Trump seemed to wield the language of that growing disgruntled group who felt displaced by the election of a man of color with ideas that threatened the long-standing status quo. Trump spoke of immigrants from Mexico by saying, "They're bringing drugs. They're bringing crime. They're rapists" (Trump, 2015).

"BUILD THE WALL!" (a cry to close the border and prevent immigration) became a popular chant associated with his campaign. I personally never thought this type of rhetoric would ever stand. But it did, and Donald Trump was narrowly elected the forty-fifth president of the United States, beating former Secretary of State Hillary Rodham Clinton, the first woman nominee from a major US political party.

Once in office, President Trump immediately rolled back progress in gender-inclusive policies. He banned trans soldiers from serving in the military. He rolled back Obama's guidance on LGBTQIA+ best practices in schools. He also called for a ban on immigrants from countries like Haiti and what he called "shithole" African countries (Fram & Lemire, 2018). Trump also called to repeal the ACA, which had produced equitable healthcare options for millions of Americans. Under his administration, he appointed three conservative Supreme Court justices, increasing the conservative majority to a 6–3 advantage. This conservative leverage ultimately led to the overturning of a woman's federal right to abortions in the *Dobbs v. Jackson*

Women's Health Organization (2022) decision that overturned *Roe v. Wade* (1973) in 2022.

After only one term as president, the US had a change of heart regarding the direction President Trump was taking the country. He lost the 2020 election to Vice President Joe Biden. Bennet and Bergan (2020) of the *New York Times* cited the key indicators of Trump's loss as the challenges he faced in dealing with the COVID-19 crisis. While Trump provided some support to mitigate the crisis experienced by the US during the pandemic shutdown, he lost support over how he handled it. Some critics also believed that Trump was obsessed with personal grievances (Bennet & Bergan, 2020), highlighting that his alienating, divisive rhetoric did not play favorably with crucial demographics such as elderly and college-educated suburbanites. After losing the presidency, Trump was accused of inciting an attack on the US Capitol on January 6, 2021. The goal, as we understand it now, was to interrupt the joint session of the US Congress and block the confirmation of the presidential election results. Among many other indictments, Trump was charged with conspiracy to defraud the United States of America with misinformation about election results and the obstruction of the certification of the 2020 election results (Congressional Review Service, 2023). Trump notoriously left the White House without attending President Biden's inauguration (Rascoe, 2021).

With four years of President Biden's administration came an attempt to reverse these changes and to reopen equitable opportunities for some marginalized populations. As one of his first official acts in office, President Biden issued a racial equity executive order to address barriers to underserved communities. He also responded to COVID-19 with the American Rescue Plan (ARP), which relieved marginalized communities by supporting small businesses and providing tax credits. As a part of the ARP, Elementary and Secondary School Emergency Relief (ESSER) grants were dispatched to help schools recover from the impact of COVID-19. President Biden's administration also adopted aggressive loan forgiveness programs for public servants and those with low incomes. The Biden administration reversed Trump's military ban on transgender individuals.

However, Donald Trump was reelected after President Biden abruptly ended his presidential campaign in the summer of

2024, leaving Vice President Kamala Harris three months to campaign against him. The November election season also yielded a conservative majority in the US House of Representatives and Senate. With this election win and the conservative-leaning Supreme Court, many speculate significant disruptions in equity work.

Bill Barrow (2024) of the Associated Press outlines his projections of what we can expect after President Donald Trump returns to the White House for his second term. First and foremost, Trump has promised an end to anything related to diversity, equity, and inclusion (DEI) that uses federal funding. This elimination is slated to roll back the Biden administration's more robust interpretation of Title IX protections for transgender students. President Biden went a step beyond the Obama administration's guidance by proposing regulations that expressly prohibit discrimination against trans students. Trump will push to recognize only two genders while banning transgender athletes from women's sports.

The incoming Trump administration has also vowed to eliminate the federal Department of Education. He plans to prohibit teacher tenure, terminate diversity programs, and restrict the use of Critical Race Theory in K-12 education (Barrow, 2024). Trump intends to redirect higher education funding to a tuition-free online American Academy. The administration will use federal funding sanctions to reduce "woke" programs that address the needs of marginalized students.

Beyond these concerning promises that will curtail or outright eliminate equity efforts, Donald Trump has also pledged to initiate the massive deportation of undocumented and even naturalized immigrants (Barrow, 2024). To reduce immigration, he plans to institute restrictive entry policies and end birthright citizenship. This action will impact students born in the US who have undocumented parents. Moreover, women's healthcare rights may become even more restrictive. With *Roe v. Wade* (1973) already overturned, the Trump administration may limit access to FDA-approved abortion pills. Doctors may also have more judgment restrictions imposed on them when addressing abortions needed due to medical emergencies.

Ultimately, ideological and political shifts in election results since 2008 have called equitable outcomes for marginalized people in the US into question. On the heels of the Obama administration and the beginning of Trump's administration, I was the inaugural equity administrator in a large school district in 2016. I worked to facilitate more equitable outcomes for students and staff. The Equity Empowerment Continuum was born using the political curiosity Ms. Ivanovich instilled in me, my academic preparation, and my practical experience challenging resistance. Regardless of the political tide, leaders in all professions will be tasked with how to lead under what could be highly restrictive, inequitable mandates. This book provides a nuanced schema to help empower you to advocate for equitable outcomes amidst challenging realities.

How This Book Is Structured

This book examines how to address issues of marginalization in educational settings. However, the concepts in this book can be applied across all kinds of organizations, large or small, business or otherwise. It is a teaching tool examining how people and organizations have succeeded and failed when confronting marginalization and how those lessons can be applied to K-12 schools. Many of the topics and examples come from those schools. Others come from the world of business. A wide range of topics are discussed, and the many examples demonstrate the ongoing struggle to obtain equity for everyone across all professions. Readers are encouraged to reflect deeply on their own dispositions and practices by scrutinizing them through the lens of these real-life scenarios. This book leans heavily on examples from recent and historical world and national events, my own experiences, and specific examples related to addressing inequities within the school context.

Typically, a deductive approach is used to solve most problems. People start by identifying solutions to address the problem. As they implement the solutions, they encounter new challenges trying to address the initial problem. Ultimately, they must address these new challenges while still focusing on the initial problem. This book takes a more inductive approach. First, you acknowledge the difficulties you may encounter as you address a problem. You explore those difficulties and why they are hard. Once you understand the potential difficulties, you act using the EEC framework. Because of this, I have organized each of the chapters in an inductive fashion: first, I will acknowledge the problems that each chapter seeks to explore, then I will use the framework to discuss potential solutions.

FOUNDATION

The introduction and chapters 1 and 2 are the foundation for understanding the Equity Empowerment Continuum, which is the primary tool for understanding equity action and inaction in this book. People naturally want to know what to do about inequity without understanding the dynamics behind the actions they choose to take. However, the introduction explains why such a tool is needed to empower individuals and groups to pursue equitable outcomes in the face of resistance. Chapter 2 introduces the foundational pieces of that decision-making. Chapter 1 introduces and explores your ICE-T (identity, context, experiences, and the timing factor), which describes and informs your capacity to execute actions in equitable ways.

PHASES

Chapters 3–6 explain the four phases of the Equity Empowerment Continuum. These phases are fluid and changeable based on how you want to empower yourself to make more equitable decisions within your context. Your actions within each phase contribute to the overall outcome for your organization.

IDENTIFIERS

Each phase is defined by real-life historical and contemporary examples that illustrate the phase's most salient features, whether they arise as behaviors, actions, or beliefs. These examples are primarily drawn from the world of K-12 education but also include examples from the broader culture. While the main audience for this book is educators, many other professionals will be able to apply this content to their field, just as educators will be able to learn from the examples in business and popular culture. The identifiers do not define who you are as a person but can help you identify areas where your actions could be contradictory to your intent. These reflective features are meant to move you along the EEC.

PHASE VIGNETTES

At the close of each phase chapter, the reader is provided with a vignette that features the phase's identifiers. These vignettes feature fictitious individuals and situations, but they are based on real people and events. At the close of the vignette, an analysis is offered to explain how the individual and their team can push through to improve their approach to equity.

PROBING QUESTIONS

Questions throughout the book prompt readers to reflect on their own attitudes and actions regarding equity and empowerment. Practical questions strategically peppered throughout encourage readers to engage actively with the material, fostering a more profound exploration of their personal and professional spheres within the context of equity and empowerment.

END-OF-CHAPTER QUESTIONS

At the end of each chapter, the reader is asked a series of questions that can be answered individually or with a team.

Acknowledgments

To my family: Mom, thank you for giving me life and many valuable lessons. Dad and Gwen, I appreciate your life's journey together. Dad, thank you for helping me take a calculated risk to achieve this monumental goal. Britty, thanks for taking me to the coffee shop to kick this whole thing off and being the family's first book author. Shawn, thanks for loving and supporting Britty. Tanya, thanks for being a sounding board for so many ideas. Brandi, thank you for always being my cheerleader. To my nieces and nephew, Naima, Zora, and Alexander, TT Tish adores you and can't wait to see what you become in this world!

To my dear grandparent ancestors: Eddie, Evia, John, and Virginia, I stand on their shoulders. "Bringing the gifts that my ancestors gave, I am the dream and the hope of the slave. I rise. I rise. I rise."—Maya Angelou

To Derute Consulting Cooperative: You believed in me and my vision. I appreciate your support. Thank you, Decoteau I., for dreaming deep, wide, and always tall. To Liz D., thank you for your favorite coffee shop's multiple writing dates and thoughtful reflections.

To Rich H., thank you for reading my ideas when they were a chaotic mess. Thank you for the encouragement to keep going. "Anything is possible with a PhD from UW-Madison!"

To Rich M. IV, this book was impossible without your influence and support. You are blessed because you are a blessing to others.

To Bianca W., thank you for helping me organize my initial thoughts for this book.

To Sister Mary D., thank you for reading my work and the many discussions that helped refine my ideas.

To the Corwin Press editorial staff, Megan B., Lucas S., and Dan A., thank you for believing in me and pushing me to do my best work.

My academic giants: Judy A., Cynthia D., Gloria L. B., and Linda T., I am because you are.

My academic mentors: Gary A., Frank B., Colleen C., Jerlando J., Catherine L., Susan M., Gail S., Raji S., and George T.

My academic colleagues: Noelle A., Barbara B., Karen B., Lisa B., Thandeka C., Terrance G., Mark G., Cosette G., Dana G., Sonya D. H., Madeline H., Frank H., Gennella J., Tom J., Muhammad K., Tori M., Patrice Mc., Laura Mc., April P. H., Sharon R., Jim S., Martin S., Regina S., Chris T., Natalie T., and Terri W.

My big brother mentor, Lonnie A., you believed in my life when I wasn't sure. Thank you for gently nurturing my leadership over all these years.

My practitioner mentors: Betty C., Kathy G., Lafayette G., Janie H., Karen J., Marty L., Jack L., Catherine M., Ken M., Mondell M., and Jim S.

My work little sisters, La Tasha F. and Teaira Mc., thank you for helping me hone and pilot the EEC.

My practitioner colleagues: Jane A., Natalie A., Tonya A., Althea B., Felice B., Janet B., Nuntiata B., Kanika B., Juan B., Gina B., Matthew B., Tina B., Melissa B. T., Alina C., Alvin C., David C., Keith C., Myrte C., Nicole C., Tanzanique C., Joseph D., Nate D., Angela F., Eric G., Cathy G., Leon G., Lynn G., Toknoka G., Anesia H., Angela H., April H., Janel H., Joe'Mar H., LaShawnda H., Nebritt H., Ryan H., Reginald I., Jon J., Nicole J., Mama Agnes J., Angelique J.C., Derrick J., Matt J., Brian J., Ophelia K., Jenny K., Annie K., Jenny L., Chad M., Demond M., Neva M., Paul M., Stephanie M., Theresa M., Carol Mc., Elnore Mc., Stanley Mc., Andy N., Carletta N., Greg O., Candice O., Chris O., Rose P., Andre R., Derrick R., LaNelle R., Angelena S., April S., James S., Jackie S., Kellie S., Marc S., Regina S., Rochelle S., Ronald S. III, Christine T., Debbie T., Maurice T., Jineen T., Floyd W., Larry W., Lucas W., Tonja W., and Zeeland W.

My Birthday Club: Monique A., Lisa G., Tabia J., and Denise P., my A-1s from Day-1.

My college "siblings": Brandon D., Benn J., and Bridget Mc.

My sorors of Sigma Gamma Rho Sorority, Inc. Special acknowledgments to Distant Unity: #1 Delechia J., #3 Lacritia S., #4 Karen W., and #5 Necole M. My specials: Rasheeda L., Nailah C., Davina P., Moya B., Nzinga K., Bridget W., and Sasha B. My Sigma Moms: Wanda A., Jerrilynn F., and Tammy G. R.

My godparents: Raoufa H. and Baseer H.

My CEO Prayer Closet, led by Donna H. I. Special thanks to Marcella M. and Mom Betty.

My Sister2Sister group, led by Brenda P.

PUBLISHER'S ACKNOWLEDGMENTS

Corwin gratefully acknowledges the contributions of the following reviewers:

Sean Beggin
Associate Principal
Anoka-Hennepin Secondary Technical Education Program
Anoka, MN

Dr. Ray Boyd
Principal
Dayton Primary School
Perth, Western Australia

Dr. Ken Darvall
Principal
Tema International School
Tema, Ghana

Ronda Gray
Clinical Associate Professor in the School of Education
University of Illinois Springfield
Springfield, IL

Melissa Miller
Science Educator
Randall G. Lynch Middle School
Farmington, AR

Lena Marie Rockwood
High School Assistant Principal
Revere Public Schools
Revere, MA

Gaby Scelfo
English Teacher
Academy of the Sacred Heart
Grand Coteau, LA

About the Author

Photo credit: Kalida N. Williams

Latish C. Reed has a career that spans over two decades as a college admissions counselor, teacher, teacher-leader, school administrator, assistant professor of leadership, and organizational equity leader. She served as the inaugural equity administrator in a large school district, where she led equity policy development and professional learning to support districtwide improvement. Beyond education, Dr. Reed has shared her expertise with corporate, healthcare, and government professionals, consulting on critical equity issues to foster inclusive environments across a variety of sectors.

I dedicate this book to my SONshine, Zion.

Because of you, I want to make the world a better place. Keep running fast and far.

Love, Mom

Introduction

Do the Right Thing, a classic movie by Spike Lee, burst onto the scene in 1989 to a barrage of controversy. I was a rising high school senior who was raised in a pretty strict home where I could not go to R-rated movies. However, I was curious about the movie because of the controversy surrounding it. Even before its release, the movie's subject matter generated polarizing debate. Some were nervous that the movie would cause riots in urban Black and Brown neighborhoods. Denaby (1989) wrote a review in *New York Magazine* that predicted that the movie would incite Black and Brown people to violence. He said, "If Spike Lee is a commercial opportunist, he is also playing with dynamite in an urban playground. The response to the movie could get away from him."

The movie climax shows a white police officer killing a young Black man in front of neighbors. This happens after the police are called to break up a disturbance between the young man, his friends, and a white business owner. The officers struggle to subdue the large, dark-skinned Black man. Finally, one officer is able to put him in a chokehold with his baton. Despite the crowd's pleas to let him go, the officer keeps his grip tight around the man's neck. Several police officers form a barrier between the majority Black and Brown onlookers as they watch his body go limp. After neighbors watch the murder in real-time, the neighborhood erupts in an uprising.

Following the movie's release, no actual riots or uprisings were reported. In fact, years later, Lee would express his outrage that critics would even suggest that Black and Brown communities would riot because of watching a film (*The Guardian*, n.d.). Even though there was fear and disdain for the film at that time, others praised it for its candid portrayal of racial tensions of the time. Gene Siskel and Roger Ebert (n.d.), among the most famous and respected movie critics of the era, ranked the movie number one for 1989 and one of the top ten movies of the decade.

The following year, I was a college freshman who embraced my newfound freedom. I rented and watched *Do the Right Thing* and several other forbidden movie titles on my VHS player. Few movies would have the lasting impression that this film had on me. The movie provided a needed and textured context for reflecting upon the complex nature of race relations in diverse communities. It showed conflict and compassion while giving me a tangible piece of art to interrogate my own views and experiences with race as a young, Black woman on a predominately white campus.

Fast forward to May 25, 2020, Memorial Day, when the entire world was shut down in some fashion. I was stuck in the house with my eighth grade son whose school had worked hard to provide as much educational coherence as possible to families because we had all been thrust into the COVID-19 pandemic. While I, along with my family and friends, was anxious about the uncertainties of the virus's impact, I was somewhat enjoying the different pace of life. Like almost everyone else, I watched movies, made way too many home-cooked meals and desserts, and increased my social media engagement to two other platforms.

On the evening of May 25th, those new social media pages began to show images of a neighborhood in distress. I saw that another unarmed Black man, George Floyd, had died because of an interaction with the police in Minneapolis, MN. To avoid mental and physical anxiety, I had learned that as police brutality and killings of unarmed Black and Brown people became more publicized, I had to monitor what I took in from both social and network media. However, with the pandemic in full swing, any significant event would attract an extraordinary amount of attention. So, I started to read the early reports. At first, the official news outlets reported that George Floyd was resisting arrest, and that he had a medical crisis and died in police custody. These seemed to be the facts, but according to social media, there was much more to this story.

On social media, I saw reports that an officer had held his knee to Floyd's neck until he died. I was stunned. Within days, the national media outlets also began to report the same thing. Then, videos and pictures of the officer with his knee on Floyd's neck began surfacing. There also seemed to be an actual cell phone video that had been captured by a high school student who was passing by. She ended up posting it on social media and that is how I was able to see it. I read what had happened, but I could not watch the video in its entirety. However, I did see a few images of the neighborhood residents that had assembled and watched the murder in real time.

The more details became available, the more this tragedy reminded me of the devastating climax scene of *Do the Right Thing*. The pictures released of officers instructing the crowd to stay back as Officer Derek Chauvin had his knee on Floyd's neck mirrored the events in the movie. People were barricaded from where they saw inhumanity take place in real time. Just as in the movie, the people had looks of horror on their faces as George Floyd was murdered in plain sight (Salter, 2021). At the time of Chauvin's trial, those who were there that fateful day described people yelling at officers to stop and becoming agitated when they realized Floyd had become unresponsive. It was the same as in the climactic scene of the movie, where everyone is in a daze after the victim is removed by the police.

The main difference was that in the movie, the neighborhood immediately erupted in a flame of uprisings. People began to destroy and set property on fire. But the people in the real-life Minneapolis neighborhood dispersed. They reemerged in social and national news outlets to tell the world of the unjust murder they witnessed in broad daylight. The power of their cell phone recordings and eye-witness testimony set off a global "awakening" about hard truths that marginalized people had been sharing for centuries.

REFLECTION

How does art reflect and influence real-life events, particularly in terms of social justice and human experiences? Which pieces of art, films, or music have had a significant influence on your understanding of race relations, injustice, or activism?

(Continued)

(Continued)

Source: Entertainment Pictures / Alamy

Source: Associated Press/Pool Court TV

TOP: In Spike Lee's 1989 film, *Do The Right Thing,* Mookie (Spike Lee), Sal (Danny Aiello), Vito (Richard Edson), and Pino (John Turturro) stand in shock outside of Sal's Famous Pizzeria after witnessing the police killing of Radio Raheem (Bill Nunn).

BOTTOM: On May 25, 2020, bystanders in a Minneapolis neighborhood looked on in shock as they witnessed the police killing of George Floyd.

In that moment, reality mirrored art. But the art was based on a reality that has known slavery and racial injustice for centuries, on a reality that allows some lives to matter less than others, and on a reality that encourages the perpetuation of racism and racial violence in its most important systems and institutions. During this time, my personal and professional experiences as a middle-aged Black woman merged, and I witnessed what I believed would be a real social and cultural shift. In my career as a teacher, scholar, educational leader, and consultant, my goal has always been to advocate and create change for traditionally marginalized individuals and groups of people. I thought, "Now the whole world understands, and we will get the justice we seek!"

That moment has passed. It has been just a few short years since the tragedy of George Floyd's murder, but many of the challenges that we faced before have resurfaced with even more barriers to overcome. As the landscape changes and Diversity, Equity, and Inclusion (DEI) efforts come under more criticism, it has become increasingly important for individuals to consider how they will continue to advocate for marginalized individuals and groups in the face of this resistance.

This book aims to build a bridge for people so they can move from ideas to tangible actions. Using the Equity Empowerment Continuum framework, I share lessons learned as a school practitioner, researcher, and the inaugural equity leader in a large organization to help readers ground their decision-making and actions, so they are oriented toward more equitable outcomes.

In 2016, I began as an inaugural equity administrator in a large school district with about seventy thousand students and an estimated eight thousand five hundred employees. I came to this role with a strong education in equity-based school leadership from the University of Wisconsin-Madison. I also spent several years as a professor and researcher teaching how to be an equitable leader. I offer both theoretical and practical insights into addressing equity within the work setting, as well as details from my personal journey.

That journey begins with navigating my ICE-T (identity, context, experiences, and timing) and employing that knowledge to advocate for equitable change in different settings and situations. Next, using personal and professional vignettes and authentic historical and contemporary examples, I put forth the Equity Empowerment Continuum (EEC) using black, white, and shades of gray to discuss and analyze various professional or personal actions or lack thereof that can lead to change on different levels. *The Complexities of Equity* offers a new perspective to navigating current challenges in implementing more equitable opportunities and structures for those who need more to succeed. The last chapter is a call to action for readers to lean into their spheres of influence to lead authentic change in their workplace and personal lives.

The world will continue to grapple with how different people from different walks of life coexist. This is an opportunity for the reader to reflect upon how they will contribute to making that world a better place for all.

DIVERSITY, EQUITY & INCLUSION (DEI) AT WORK

Once a fuller picture of what happened on that fateful day in Minneapolis emerged, global protests erupted. People flooded the streets worldwide to demand justice for George Floyd and the countless other victims of racial brutality and killing. It was almost as if the whole world said in that moment, "We will no longer turn a blind eye." With that came an awareness of the need to examine where people worked. Discussions about and examinations of Diversity, Equity, and Inclusion (DEI) became commonplace in the world of work.

But before discussing how DEI work has trended, I want to define equity, its companion terms (diversity and inclusion), and its ultimate goal to address life's "isms." CEO and author Catherine Mattice offered a basic equity definition in an article written for LinkedIn. According to Mattice (2023), "Equity refers to the fair and just treatment of all individuals, regardless of their diverse characteristics. It means ensuring that everyone has equal access to opportunities and resources and an equal chance to succeed. That means barriers preventing some individuals from succeeding must also be removed."

My definition is even simpler: *Instead of making sure everyone has the same or equal resources, opportunities, and/or support, equity means insuring they have what they need at the level they need it.*

REFLECTION

How do you define equity, personally and within your professional setting?

A common example: Instead of giving everyone the same pair of shoes, people need different shoes based on their foot size, purpose, climate, fashion sense, and other essential accommodations. You would not want someone with a size seven shoe who was going to a fancy gala to be given the same shoe as a person with a size twelve foot who works on a farm. Shoes would need to be tailored for different individuals in various contexts.

Another example is food portions for a growing child. I have been a single mom for most of my son's life. Food is an important part of our relationship. If ever my son is not hungry, there must be a serious problem. The amount of food I prepare is different from what I need, as he requires larger portions to accommodate his body. One staple food in our house is fish. When he was three, he would eat half a piece. Making fish for an eighteen-year-old man requires a minimum of four pieces with the option for seconds. I would get laughed out of my own home if I put a half piece of fish on his plate today. Like many Americans, I often struggle with maintaining an appropriate weight. As someone who could spare a couple of pieces of fish for my growing son, it really is about my willpower to make sure I do not eat more than I need and make sure he has seconds.

The term *equity* is often grouped with *diversity* and *inclusion*. Murray (2023) describes DEI work as "a three-pronged approach, which is why these terms are being used in so many of these new job titles." In this sense, **diversity** aims to "remove bias and barriers so that a company's workforce can reflect the heterogeneity of the communities it operates in." The strategy is to focus on hiring nontraditional candidates and ensuring they are compensated and offered the appropriate opportunities they need to thrive within the organization. **Inclusion** basically means that the organization invites and welcomes the ideas and attributes that arise as the organization diversifies.

Fernandes (2021), senior director of employer brand and culture and head of DEI Practice at Blu Ivy Group, also highlights the use of the "B" word, **belonging**. The money spent on DEI work often focuses on measuring DEI metrics, while missing the critical aspect of how people feel they belong in an organization. She suggests that we bring "together DEI and engagement experts to focus on DEI and engagement in a more holistic and effective way."

While the concepts of DEI seem simple, they have proven to be difficult to implement. For instance, those who always get what they need within an organization may fear that they will stop having their needs met as a result of DEI efforts. They fear having the extra they may be accustomed to receiving cut off as well. As Teresa Hopke (2022) noted in a *Forbes* article, nearly 70 percent of white men "report feeling 'forgotten' by diversity, equity, and inclusion efforts." They cite concerns about losing promotions or other benefits they might have expected before such efforts were implemented. Some white men resist Diversity, Equity, and Inclusion (DEI) trainings because they feel blamed or shamed for their privileges. It highlights the zero-sum bias, where they perceive that giving opportunities to marginalized groups means fewer opportunities for them, leading to a desire for equality but with resistance to perceived preferential treatment.

People who have been accustomed to having their needs met (and beyond) typically make it difficult to "do the right thing" to achieve more equitable outcomes for others. This is where the challenges begin, but certainly not where they end.

From this point, in this book, I will mostly refer to Diversity, Equity and Inclusion, and other related titles as *equity*. This term is used as an umbrella term to capture the various titles used to describe DEI.

EQUITY AND LIFE'S "'ISMS" AND "OBIAS"

Those who resist equity tend to focus on maintaining the status quo, such as ensuring that those who do not have what they need are kept from getting it. The "isms" and "obias" of life have become the major barrier to creating more equitable outcomes for individuals and groups of marginalized people, specifically, "isms" and "obias" like racism, ableism, sexism, classism, homophobia, xenophobia, and nationalism. These describe a few of the ways people think about or treat others based on their identities. "Isms" are societal systems that marginalize others, while "obias"— conscious or unconscious prejudices—influence people's judgment and behavior toward others in an unfair way.

These impacts happen on a personal, organizational, and societal level. As a Black woman, I primarily face racism and sexism. Throughout this book, I will offer different ways to address the "isms" and "obias" of life, but especially within the educational context. Those seeking justice are committed to doing the right thing by working with both people who share their identity and those who do not.

Equity efforts have become a way for many to pursue justice in a variety of institutions, like corporations, schools, government agencies, healthcare, and the criminal justice system. With equity being popularized, society is thinking more critically about past inabilities to obtain equity for all. Obstacles to achieving such equity persist. As reported by the Equal Opportunity Employment Commission and *Harvard Business Review*, many people fear that if they were to admit or name their organization's failures and start asking tough questions, they could be targeted in a way that threatens their job security (Feldblum & Lipnic, 2016; Zheng, 2020). That is how equity work becomes political and ultimately marginalized.

EQUITY: THE EBBS AND FLOWS

Equity has become a part of most organization's standard operating procedures, particularly after the disparate impact of COVID-19 and the global resistance to violence against unarmed Black men and women displayed in 2020. As a past equity leader, my LinkedIn timeline is consistently flooded with organizations, companies, and institutions posting DEI chief, director, or manager positions to ensure that their organization is in line with the cultural shifts that are taking place. Maurer (2020) of The Society of Human Resource Management reported a spike in such roles following the watershed protests against the murder of George Floyd at the hands of the police. This growth is visible in the United States of America and can be seen globally. LinkedIn revealed that within the last five years, equity positions in Europe, the Middle East, and Africa have experienced a massive growth spurt, both at middle management and senior-level positions.

However, the momentum has slowed. In August 2023, Andrea Hsu (2023), labor and workplace correspondent for NPR, reported on corporate equity cutbacks:

> Economic pressures have led companies to pull back, cutting DEI jobs... alongside other human resources roles. Since last July, Indeed has seen DEI job postings drop by 38%.
>
> And then in June, in another blow to diversity advocates, the Supreme Court rejected the use of race-conscious admissions in higher education, setting off predictions that corporate policies around diversity will soon meet the same fate.

According to a LinkedIn study, the demand for chief diversity and inclusion officers increased by 168.9 percent between 2019 to 2022, but overall opportunities for these positions actually dropped by 4.51 percent between 2021 and 2022 (Anders, 2023). The same report details waning interest in diversity and inclusion due to recession concerns, fatigue, and high turnover rates. While diversity-related positions in this area ballooned, many who obtained them reported that they lacked the appropriate resources and supports for success.

This reduction could be connected to political backlash and economic constraints. In June 2023, Governor Greg Abbott of Texas signed a bill into law that bans DEI offices at public universities. This monumental action makes Texas the second state to take such drastic actions against equity efforts, with Florida being the first. This change means that DEI offices, programs, and training at these institutions will cease to exist. The students and staff who were empowered by these efforts will be left completely without recourse, and those who led DEI efforts at the university will be left without jobs.

Anti-equity measures have not stopped there. In June 2023, the US Supreme Court overturned an important law that provided more equitable outcomes in college admissions. Less than sixty years ago, US colleges and universities were officially desegregated with the Civil Rights Act of 1964 and the Higher Education Act of 1965. Even after the codification of desegregation, barriers for people of color persisted. It has been documented that BIPOCs have been negatively impacted by racism and discrimination in college admissions. Yet, the *Students for Fair Admissions, Inc. v. President and Fellows of Harvard College* has eliminated race as a consideration in college admissions. The implications of this decision will have a long-lasting impact on college admissions for BIPOCs.

REFLECTION

In broader society, how have you witnessed equity efforts persist or wane in the last decade? How does that compare to your personal or professional context?

GET SET! ARE WE READY?

An organization's readiness for equity work is wide-ranging. In many cases, organizations have technical goals for achieving more equitable outcomes, but they lack an understanding of the complex issues they face, and struggle with the discomfort of vested stakeholders. Hiring equity leaders can be a good starting point for an organization, company, or institution. At the same time, equity leaders can become the "sage on the stage" responsible for moving an agenda with financial and human resources but limited to making minimal changes. From my observations and experiences, to attain true change, it is up to leaders and individuals to enact equity within their spheres of control and influence.

In these times, most educational institutions have considered or already initiated strategic planning and professional development in equity. As previously mentioned, this work may be contested depending on the state's political climate. This is not a "how to" equity strategy book. The book's intent is to help strengthen the resolve of individuals and groups to implement the needed actions to bring about equitable change. This book can assist readers in discovering a starting place within your sphere of influence and control, as well as a pathway to the sustainability of equity efforts.

PROGRAMS, POLICIES, AND PROCEDURES DO NOT CHANGE PRACTICES. PEOPLE DO!

In May 2020, the spotlight on DEI was heightened as the world, workplaces, and schools struggled to make sense of the recorded murder of George Floyd. Many people who had always seen themselves as good, decent, and fair human beings wanted to uncover deeper truths about race, police brutality, and systemic racism, and they searched for ways to learn more amid the COVID-19 pandemic shutdown. As many people reached for resources to gain new understanding, they bought *How to Become Antiracist* by Ibram X. Kendi (2019) and *White Fragility: Why It's So Hard for White People to Talk About Racism* by Robin Diangelo (2018). In June 2020, Kendi's book became a top seller in multiple major outlets (*New York Times* best seller list, *USA Today*, and Amazon). Similarly, *White Fragility* experienced multiple weeks as a *New York Times* best seller. Both books address race. This opened the door to many books and professional development training programs across all industries on topics related to uncovering and correcting long-standing societal injustices.

While I was equipped with a strong academic and research background, I quickly learned that practical tools were needed to support an entire organization on a journey of understanding and implementing the changes needed to increase equitable outcomes for students, families, and the community we served. One of the most useful tools in my work was *Courageous Conversations About Race* (CCAR) by Glenn Singleton (2021). Members from the district's Positive Behavioral Interventions and Supports (PBIS) team initially did book studies on this book and introduced it to me. With their help, we were able to arrange state-sponsored training. It was an extremely impactful training. Ultimately, we were able to get some central service administrators, school board, and other community members trained on the book's protocol. After I left the role, the district adopted a train-the-trainer model, and all certified and classified district employees are now required to undergo training sessions on the CCAR framework.

CCAR (Singleton, 2021) offers a healthy way to engage in productive conversations about race. The most recent edition addresses deeper inequities exposed after the pandemic shutdown. This book contains the original components of the CCAR protocol which includes a compass, four agreements, and six conditions that provide a foundation for positive dialogue. It is written in an accessible style that anyone can understand and is applicable to settings even beyond education. The compass is an excellent way to understand that all people come from different vantage points into this work. Additionally, the agreements are a structuring tool for setting a foundational stage for valuable conversations that can potentially be sensitive.

REFLECTION

What are the most useful tools you have at your disposal to address inequities within your work setting?

As powerful as this training is, if individual people are not committed to the process or leaders do not hold their staff accountable, no changes are made in practice. My mother always said to me as I grew up, "More of the same, produces no change." The Equity Empowerment Continuum is a tool that can help people determine their capacity to "do the right thing." I found people who were resistant to ideas of equity were also resistant to the training. Some people walked away from the trainings and follow-ups and never used the protocol. However, they "checked the box" and met the requirement by participating in the sessions.

After all the training, discussions, and debates about how to create a more equitable environment, the real area of focus is about what the individual or team of individuals will *do*. This book will help you determine to what extent you and others are willing to "do the right thing" to bring the change you seek to impact.

CHAPTER 1

Sipping on Your ICE-T

Your Identity, Context, and Experience Matter

I have taught several equity courses that specifically deal with issues related to leading equity in schools and districts. When I teach, my goal is to engage students in course content that addresses the inequities. We also discuss life's "isms," and "obias." As described in the introduction, "isms" and "obias," such as racism, sexism, and xenophobia, are barriers that suppress efforts to create equity for marginalized people. Sometimes, it is difficult to have conversations about sensitive and controversial topics. To prepare my students to authentically engage in class, we first spend time understanding ourselves and the others in the room. We explore each other's backgrounds and experiences. If there are twenty-three students in the class, I say, "This course has twenty-three individualized prerequisites. And no one has taken anyone else's prerequisites." In other words, an individual's background impacts how they think about and address inequity and life's "isms" and "obias."

After those same students graduate from their preparation program, they will become district and school leaders. Then, the task becomes to decide how to adequately address the inequities, "isms," and "obias" of life that are ever-present in schools. For this reason, before we talk about how individuals decide how to act, we must explore who individuals are.

UNIQUE DATA SOURCES

As a researcher, I have always sought different ways to collect and use data to discuss complex challenges. The data used to construct the Equity Empowerment Continuum (EEC) comes from the autoethnographic tradition. The EEC is a reflection framework I developed based on my experiences in both the academy and in the field. While there are several ways to describe autoethnography, Chang (2016) describes it as the understanding of self, others, and culture. The methodology connects the researcher with the culture, political atmosphere, and broader society that they exist within, but the autoethnographer is the primary source of data. Synder (2015) distinguishes autoethnography from other forms of personal narrative by noting that autoethnography goes beyond personal stories to analyze culture. In this book, I analyze culture and the broader context of my work by using my own experiences with historical and contemporary events so that readers can identify and reconsider what those events meant in their lives.

In addition, I draw from data that Dillard (2000) calls "life notes," which refer broadly to constructed personal narratives such as "letters, journal entries, reflections, poetry, music, and other artful forms of data" (p. 664). I used my "life notes" to create the EEC framework so that I could navigate equity based on my lived experiences, reflections, and current events, which is especially important because, as Dillard notes (2000), mainstream research does not always reflect the lived experiences of Black women. Therefore, any singular story we can offer contributes to the literature in its own right and as a counternarrative.

SIPPING ON YOUR ICE-T: YOUR IDENTITY, CONTEXT, EXPERIENCE, AND TIMING MATTER

Before we discuss the Equity Empowerment Continuum, it is important to understand the underlying foundations people have that inform their choices and decisions on action. Where do we begin? As a career educator, I love memorable acronyms to assist students' knowledge retention. Identity, context, timing, and experiences (ICE-T) are what provide the foundation for your decisions. Form 1.1 outlines the four components of your equity foundation.

FORM 1.1 • What Is Your ICE-T?

Directions: In the spaces provided below, write notes that describe your personal ICE-T (Identity, Context, Experience, and Timing).

ICE-T	DESCRIPTION
Identity	
Context	
Experience	
Timing	

These four major components all matter in your impetus to make actionable changes. As you navigate the equity landscape, some of the ICE-T factors are within your sphere of control and influence, while others are completely outside of your control. The Equity Empowerment Continuum helps you assess how you can move forward despite the complexity of this work. In other words, your ICE-T can help you "push through the shades of gray," in your equity work.

Note Regarding ICE-T: The following four sections are described out of order. I have switched the C (Context) with the E (Experience) for a better flow. I believe that a person's experiences are slightly more salient than their context.

YOUR IDENTITY MATTERS

Equity work starts with the self-exploration of your **identity**. Understanding your own identity and who you are in relation to the equity challenges you are facing is the essential starting place. As you attempt to create more equitable outcomes in your immediate life, community, and workplace, you must first understand yourself.

While the United States Declaration of Independence holds that "all men are created equal," the group of people who wrote the declaration were white, cisgendered men of middle to upper-class wealth. Three of the five men who drafted the document owned Black slaves. Even though, over time, we have changed the interpretation of the Declaration to reflect the diversity of our contemporary nation, the original language still stands. If you happen to be a poor LGBTQ woman of color, these words did not and perhaps still do not apply to you. On the other hand, if your identity is closer to the committee of five men who drafted the Declaration, you may feel affirmed and empowered. The words of our nation's founders have colored the way we all experience equality in this country. Nonetheless, your identity has caused you to experience life in a particular way, influencing your disposition.

Oftentimes, people want to jump to the solutions before identifying the problem and their self-awareness about where they stand in relationship to potential solutions. When I facilitate equity professional development workshops, people often want to get a list of things to do to change inequitable outcomes.

So, we must start with ourselves. It is much easier to turn the spotlight on everything outside of us and expose where flawed thinking or inequitable actions are taking place with respect to others. However, the first step in this process is to examine *yourself* by becoming aware of your own biases and behaviors and the ways that they contribute to inequities. Although it is extremely uncomfortable, it is essential to explore them.

An easy way to think about your identities is through a simple activity our equity team facilitates, which is called the identity pie. The identity pie is a way to show how we have specific identity pieces that make up the whole of who we are. A simple definition of "identity" is a set of characteristics that describe your essential qualities. Some examples of identity we can see include, but are not limited to, race, class, gender expression, and body type. But there are many other attributes that help define you.

To explain **cultural identities**, Hollie (2017) used an identity iceberg to explain that some of the personal characteristics we exhibit are seen, while others are not (see figure 1.1). For example, you can make a lot of assumptions about who I am based on my appearance. I am a cisgendered Black woman with a feminine gender expression. I usually wear makeup, jewelry, and sometimes a dress or skirt. I wear natural, unstraightened short hair that has gray peeking out around my face. I am of average height, but I carry more than average weight. These physical characteristics may lead one to assume a lot about who I am and what I believe.

One time, I co-facilitated a workshop with a white female colleague about identity. We wanted to mirror an activity about people's identities and the assumptions that others hold about them. To prepare, I sat opposite my colleague and asked her to erase everything that she knew about me and provide who she might think I am based on my visible identities. Even though I am a middle-class woman with a doctoral degree, she said that I looked like I could have been a sales associate at a store like Walmart or Target who lived in the inner city. While there is nothing wrong with a Black woman working at a retail outlet, I was shocked at her assessment.

I told her that she looked like she came from the suburbs and was a soccer mom. But for some reason, I assumed that she was in a bowling league. I do not consider a bowling league to go with a suburban soccer mom. At the end of the day, we *do* judge books by their covers. As such, we have to acknowledge and uncover ways to combat these inherent stereotypes. If we do not, this will impact our decision-making.

FIGURE 1.1 • Visible and Invisible Attributes

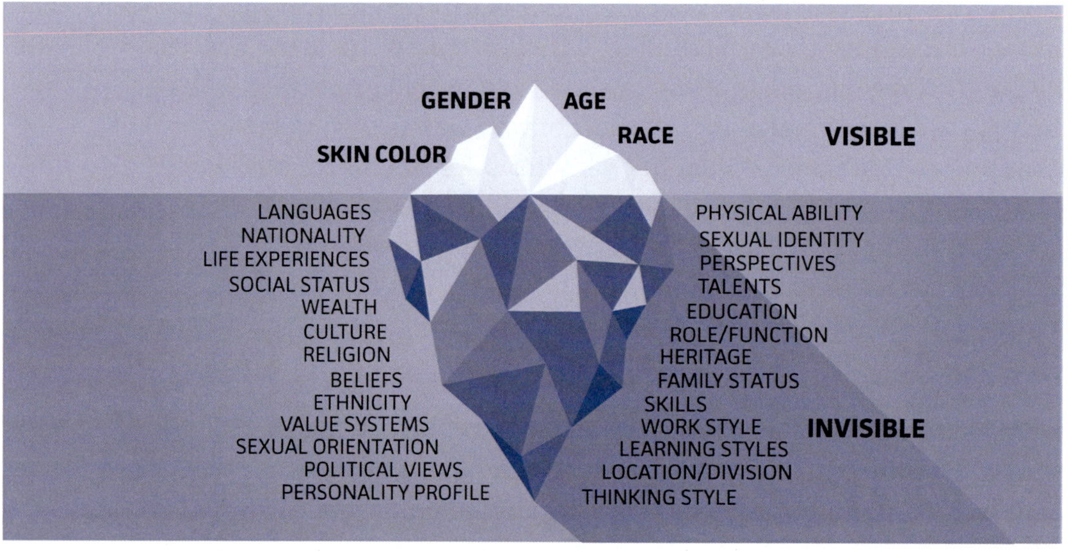

Source: Chavapong Prateep Na Thalang / Alamy

The second part of our cultural identity encompasses the visible attributes. We need to go below the water's surface to understand the invisible identities in the iceberg illustration that Hollie (2017) uses. When discussing unseen identities in the workshop, I would always reveal things about myself that were not visible. It was at this point that I would talk about living with Lupus, a chronic autoimmune disease. While many disabilities are visible, the impacts of Lupus are often hidden. The disease keeps me fatigued, which means I never feel well-rested and run out of energy throughout the day. This disease has impacted my life by affecting my joints and kidney function. It created an early onset of arthritic conditions in my fingers, knees, and elbows. Over the course of the twenty-plus years since I was diagnosed, I have experienced something called flare-ups. During flare-ups, all the symptoms are elevated, which means I experience extreme fatigue and increased pain in my joints. To get these symptoms under control, I take a daily maintenance cocktail of ten pills. One of the most helpful but dreadful medications I take is an oral steroid that causes fast and steep weight gain.

Lupus has impacted my life in many ways. First, as a single mother of a young boy, my energy levels have had to be balanced against a demanding career that requires me to be always alert and sharp. When people meet me, they would never know that as soon as I get home from work, I sometimes go to bed immediately and do not leave it until the next morning. Looking at me, people may assume that I do not exercise or monitor my diet. It is very much to the contrary. I exercise a minimum of four times per week, and I monitor my diet (for the most part, like everyone else). However, the oral steroid regimen, in combination with my consistent low-to-medium-grade level of fatigue, has created a plateau for my weight.

REFLECTION

What visible and invisible identities do you have? What assumptions do you make about people based on what you see of them? What do you get wrong? And what do people often get wrong about you?

Our identities can be a source of marginalization or privilege. In recent years, educators, coaches, and other professionals who discuss privilege and marginalization have had sanctions wielded against them for discussing such notions in public classrooms or workplaces. I am sure that a diverse population was likely not what our nation's founding fathers had in mind when they wrote "all men are created equal." But today, many majority-conservative state legislatures are passing laws that prevent teaching about the historical marginalization of certain groups of people in a factual manner.

These pieces of legislation are putting the squeeze on exploring identities, whether your own or someone else's, so as to preserve the comfort of the privileged, who often feel uncomfortable discussing what they have gained because of that privilege.

None of us want to feel bad because of anything that we have not personally done. However, if we are committed to an equity agenda, we must commit to ensuring the inclusivity that our nation's founders wrote about when they claimed the equality of all people. If we consider the "isms" and "obias" people frequently exhibit, we can understand that people's life experiences are made difficult due to the identities that they hold and the way people respond to them. It is your choice to determine to what extent you are willing to explore these identities and their relationship to the inequities we see in our society. As James Baldwin said, "We can disagree and still love each other unless your disagreement is rooted in my oppression and denial of my humanity and right to exist." The Equity Empowerment Continuum tool will directly help assess the extent of your actions towards the end goal of increased equitable outcomes.

YOUR EXPERIENCES MATTER

Our experiences help form our thoughts and dispositions. These experiences are what call us to action. In his book *Courageous Conversations About Race*, Singleton (2021) has readers explore their racial autobiography, an activity that uncovers how race has impacted their lives. In her book, Wilkinson (2021) also uses the "story of origin" as a critical starting point to understand people's capacity to act with an equity mindset. As you attempt to use your identity in this work, your experiences will emerge as a foundation for your actions.

In addition to sharing suggestions about how to navigate equity implementation, my purpose in writing this book is to share my experiences related to the identities I hold as a Black girl, young woman, and professional woman. My experience is also an extension of my ancestors and the elders who came before me. When my enslaved ancestors arrived in this country, they pushed as far as they could in each generation so that I could be who and what I am today. My maternal grandfather, Eddie Tharbs, always told me to get as much "paper as you can." What he meant was that I should pursue as many degrees and certifications as I could because he only got a third-grade education.

With a leadership career spanning over two decades, I have been an admissions counselor, teacher, teacher-leader, school administrator, charter school proposal writer, grant writer, PhD student of educational leadership and policy analysis, assistant professor of leadership, adjunct professor, district equity administrator, consultant, and speaker. While my primary focus is the education field, I have consulted with business corporations, the healthcare field, and governmental agencies on issues of diversity, equity, and inclusion. Enacting an equity agenda is needed across all organizations and institutions not only because it is the right thing to do but to ensure that the organization is not violating nondiscrimination laws. My blended background and lived experience as a Black woman navigating systems and institutions in the US also provides an important vantage point. In the next section, I will share how my experiences have shaped my pursuit of equitable outcomes.

SCHOOL EXPERIENCES

I am the oldest of four daughters. My dad was a young man who excelled throughout school and had musical talents, which led to local stardom in a regional band. Raised as the fourth eldest son in a large family of eleven children in Milwaukee, Wisconsin, my father came of age as a young Black man during the civil unrest of the 1960s. He was raised to advocate for himself and others no matter what. Through many colorful stories from my father over the years, I learned about how my father spoke truth to power even in the face of the racism he experienced.

After marrying at the age of twenty-one and having me, my dad decided to become a Jehovah's Witness, which has several specific guidelines that must be followed. For example, Jehovah's Witnesses do not celebrate holidays or recite the Pledge of Allegiance. My father made it clear to my teachers and me that I would not participate in either of these activities at school. That meant I was to be excused to the hallway when birthday treats were handed out and when the traditional "Happy Birthday" song was sung. I also went into the hallway every morning when the Pledge of Allegiance was recited. So, instead of taking a knee, I was "taking the hallway" like Colin Kaepernick would eventually take a knee, but for different reasons.

While I never formally became a Jehovah's Witness, the experience of growing up and having to stand against the status quo developed my capacity to stand on certain principles even if they are unpopular. At first, when I was in kindergarten, it was uncomfortable to be different in these ways. But, as time went on, I became comfortable being uncomfortable.

Raised in Chicago, my mother was the middle child of fourteen. Her parents were property and business owners in Black neighborhoods in Chicago. They ruled with an iron fist and, at times, probably used tactics that would now be considered abusive by today's standards. Nevertheless, my mother was a smart kid who found her way into college with the help of her oldest brother. Mom attended college in Wisconsin. This was a whole new world than she was used to in Chicago. She went from being around all Black people in her school and neighborhood to being one of the few Black students at an all-white university. College is where she would meet my father. She married him at the age of twenty to start a young family.

As my sisters and I are darker-skinned girls with kinky hair, my mom always encouraged us to wear our natural hair and braids in the 1980s, when many Black people were straightening their hair to match white standards of beauty. She even found brown band-aids called Soul-Aids because the regular flesh-color ones did not match our Brown skin.

My mother has always had a strong sense of justice, making her an outcast in most spaces. As Black girls, the message that my sisters and I always got from my mother was that we belonged anywhere we deserved or wanted to be. Despite whatever barriers white society and individuals tried to place in front of us, we learned to always stand toe-to-toe with them so that we could have access to whatever they were blatantly or covertly trying to stop us from having. We often went to stores not frequented by people of color. My mother required that we receive the same top-quality service that other shoppers received. And if we did not, she would request the manager. She would "school" them on the gap in services we received and request that we be made whole. We often left stores with discounts or extra spoils due to her advocacy. Sometimes, if we did not receive justice in the store, she would follow up with a letter to a corporate office. Even if it were months later, she would have some sort of settlement. This taught me that the race is not always given to the swift but to those who can endure it until the end. You must be strategic in the pursuit of justice. You must also prepare backup plans when your first petition is ignored or refused.

When I was of school age, I participated in a school integration social experiment after the civil rights movement. In the mid-seventies, my mother had just had my sister when I went to kindergarten. Being the "princess" I was, my mother could not fathom me walking a few blocks to the neighborhood school alone. And as the mother of a newborn, it was unreasonable that she would have to walk my new baby sister and me to school. My mom went to the school district central office to figure out how her little "princess" would get to school safely. Their solution was a bus that could take me to school in a neighboring suburb.

So, in 1977 I was bused to a neighboring, predominately white suburb for kindergarten. I remember the smell of drying paint on art projects completed by the morning kindergarteners and the graininess on the bottom of my shoes from the sandbox station when I walked past it. I also remember wondering why we had to lay down at school for a nap when we had our own beds at home.

But what I remember most from my entire time in kindergarten was that I spent most of it in the coatroom. I remember the coatroom in the fall, winter, and spring. The coatroom attire went from summer jackets to fall sweaters, winter coats, boots, mittens, hats, and scarves. It changed in the spring to cool rain boots that my parents wouldn't buy and raincoats. Then, back to summer jackets. Why did I spend such a great deal of time in the coatroom? I was sent there because most things I said or did were considered an exhibition of bad behavior. I don't quite remember all the details, but I remember being sent to the coatroom every time something happened. When my parents came to school and the teachers told them about my behavior problems, my parents were extremely surprised. It became clear that "princess" Latish did not belong in this new world with white teachers and students who were consistently misunderstanding her.

I just didn't fit. At one point, the teachers suggested to my parents that I be tested for special education because I was having an extremely hard time adjusting to school. My mother had the foresight to know that a special education label on a little Black girl who seemed to be able to interact everywhere other than school would not be a good idea. This is not to say that students who need special education services should not get them. But she knew that Black students with special education labels are more likely to be at-risk for not graduating on grade level, and that was not an option.

Fortunately, while I did not fit in, I had a few teachers I will forever be indebted to who saw my potential and did not write me off. Ms. Perkins was the elementary school music teacher who recognized that I was musical, could sing, and was extremely dramatic. She gave me solos and even suggested I take the lead in one of the grade-level musical productions. Ms. Furlong, my second-grade teacher, knew I was a tough cookie but worked very closely with my parents to help support my leadership potential. Finally, Ms. Merrigan, my sixth-grade teacher, also hung in there with me and never held anything against me. Every day was a new day. When I graduated from the University of Wisconsin-Madison with my PhD, I had a celebratory dinner at a restaurant in Madison, Wisconsin. The server informed me that I had an important phone call. When I got on the phone, Ms. Merrigan was on the line to personally congratulate me on my accomplishment. I was overwhelmed when she told me she had always known I would succeed.

Unfortunately, several other experiences led me to believe I did not belong in that school. When I was in the fourth grade, my teacher made sure that I received any and every sanction that her behavior system allowed. Students could earn green tickets that could be accumulated for opportunities to pick something from a "treasure chest" at the end of the week. Rarely did I earn green tickets. I was the recipient of yellow tickets, which reflected the poor choices or behaviors that I always seemed to be caught making in her class. At that point, I hated school. My teacher always made sure that the other students knew that Latish was different.

I remember a particular lesson about dialect that she taught. I was really into this lesson because she pointed out people talked differently in different parts of the country. She explained that people from New England had specific speech patterns and used different words than we used in the Midwest. I enjoyed the new learning until she asked me to repeat in front of the class: "May I ask you a question?"

I said, “May I ‘ax’ you a question?” No one caught it at first, so she asked me to repeat myself. I did. She then pointed out that, instead of enunciating the word “ask,” I used the word “ax.” She then incorrectly named this as an exclusive feature of a Black dialect. (The use of “ax,” or “aks” is common in many dialects and was once the preferred form printed in *Bibles* across the English-speaking world [Lindsey, 2024].). But perhaps my language pattern did exemplify Black dialect in some ways. Either way, I was embarrassed and mortified that she pointed it out in front of my classmates at nine years old. If that wasn’t enough, she announced to the class that she was seeking new ideas for more exotic dinners to make for her family. She turned to me and asked, “What did you have for dinner last night?” She looked disappointed when I said, “Baked chicken, rice, and green beans.”

In the fifth grade, when my teacher taught about slavery, she pointed out that some of the women slaves during that time went into labor in the field as they were working. They would have their babies under trees but then put the baby on their backs and continue to work. A classmate asked me in front of the entire class if I was born under a tree. My teacher said nothing as the class laughed. I have had kids surprised that the bottom of my feet and the insides of my hands were “white.” I have also been interrogated about why my hair looks the way it does or why oil needs to be added to it.

These experiences of being “othered” shaped my inherent nature to advocate for others because I know firsthand what it feels like to be on the margins, particularly in the educational setting. As these incidents occurred, my parents always stood in the gap for me. They never blindly took my side because they knew I had a spirited character that really did challenge authority. But my parents would not allow me to be railroaded into a place where I would not be able to recover or achieve my fullest potential. They believed that I had the potential to make it through this situation.

REFLECTION

What experiences of “othering” have you had that have informed your advocacy?

From an early age, I have always had a sense of justice. My mother always instilled that I must stand up for what is right. When I was a child, I watched her always stand out, always be different, and take a lot of criticism for it. My mom never shied away from any fight, big or small. This helped develop my sense of justice and advocacy for others.

COLLEGE EXPERIENCES

I attended college at a predominantly white, Catholic liberal arts university. My undergraduate experience was academically and emotionally traumatic at times. I always knew that I had what it took to graduate, but throughout the course of my time as an undergraduate, I had several experiences where I was made to question if I was good enough to graduate despite everything that had been poured into me to prepare for college.

In my first semester of college, I took the English introduction course that all freshmen were required to enroll in. We had small classes of about twenty-five students. Over the course of the semester, four or five papers were due. One of the required readings for this class was a compilation of essays. Some were from professors, but a portion of the essays came from former freshmen. My instructor would assign additional essays throughout the course as we studied writing and prepared to write the assigned papers for the semester. We also had to purchase packets of all the papers students wrote for each assignment. Part of our work was analyzing and giving feedback on our classmates' papers. In class discussions, my classmates would often raise topics that I had written about as examples of techniques they found to be exemplary. They would mention ideas like, "I really liked the way Latish provided an attention-grabbing introduction," or "Latish really used smooth transitions between different ideas." However, when I would get my paper back, I never could manage to garner an A from the professor.

Being the studious student I was, I made appointments to see my instructor to find out what I needed to do to get an A on the upcoming papers. She gave me some good feedback, but one day, she told me that she was grading me on a different level because I was such a good writer. That puzzled me because the course was a general education section, not an honors-level course. As we neared the end of the first semester, my teacher asked to speak to me after class. After everyone left, she told me that she had submitted one of my essays to be reviewed by the English department to be included in the *Freshman English Reader*, a college textbook comprised of outstanding texts written by the university's college freshmen. She just wanted me to know. She wasn't sure that it would be included, and the chances were pretty slim. Keep in mind that she gave me a B+ on the paper that I wrote, which she submitted. Lo and behold, this paper was selected for the *Freshman Reader* and was published there multiple years after that year. This was the first of many experiences where I understood that I had something to contribute that people would always want. But others would not always be willing to credit and acknowledge my gifts and talents properly. If it had not been for the TRIO Educational Opportunity Programs, designed to support students of color and first-generation students, I am not sure if I would have graduated from that university.

I am grateful that I was reaffirmed during my graduate school experiences at Alverno College in Milwaukee, Wisconsin, and the University of Wisconsin-Madison. Both places were fertile grounds for building my confidence and capacity to write in ways that led to professional and academic success. My writing has been published in some of the top academic journals in the field of education leadership. I have also written grants, securing hundreds of thousands of dollars of funding.

PROFESSIONAL CAREER EXPERIENCES

Early in my education career, I experienced some success. Following a couple of years as an admissions officer for my alma mater, I had the great fortune to become a middle school teacher in an urban school district. After three years as a classroom teacher, I worked under a gifted, innovative school administrator as an assistant principal in a school that had been "left behind." During my four years in that school, we made incredible gains that impacted the lives of many students. I was the chief proposal writer for turning the school into a district charter school, which enabled us to pursue many innovative initiatives that led to large academic improvement gains for students. I wrote and managed grants that contributed to building the capacity of our staff so that they would be culturally responsive to the students we served.

For the first ten years of my professional career as a K-12 educator and administrator, I experienced many classroom and leadership successes. I was not prepared for the major hit to my professional career that was to come. In 2014, I was denied promotion to associate professor with tenure at the university where I worked. This denial came despite strong progress over the course of my time at the institution.

The year before I was denied tenure, I ranked number two in a department of eleven colleagues. The ranking was based on publications, teaching evaluations, and service to the field, university, and local community. In five prior years of submitting annual productivity portfolios for review to the tenured members of my department, I had never been led to believe that I would not be tenured. Every year, my review feedback indicated that I was progressing adequately toward tenure.

On the day of my tenure consideration, I was asked to be present in my office while the tenured department members deliberated. I felt confident that I would receive tenure, so I sat in my office answering emails. When the meeting was over, the department chair came into my office to explain that the committee's voting results were split, which meant the decision was not to grant me tenure. I remember feeling the blood drain from my body, and I basically went numb. I don't recall much of anything he said after that. I just felt like I needed to leave immediately to pick up my son from after-school care.

After this devastating blow, I had a few colleagues, families, and friends who encouraged me to go through the appeals process, but this did not produce the reversed outcome I sought. As I watched the details unfold in this devastating situation, I realized how institutional racism, sexism, and ableism can be upheld with codified legal rules. Every attorney I contacted seemed to be connected to the university in some way. Literally, the first attorney I saw for a consultation explained that, in full disclosure, he used to work as an adjunct professor for my department teaching the school law class.

Without money or networks, I felt there was no pathway to justice. Appeal processes and protections only work if those who prosecute them are truly independent of the institutions involved or are not financially tied to them either through a paycheck or any other form of financial remuneration. Other than that, many times the very people these systems were designed to protect find themselves climbing an uphill battle with pebbles, rocks, and boulders rolling down the hill directly toward them. It takes courage to speak out against an organization you work for if you find yourself in the situation I was in or if you are a part of the organization and you recognize inequities or injustices.

Even though being denied tenure was heartbreaking, I was able to move on. However, it has been an uphill battle not letting that experience define who I am. Many people of color who experience situations like this often make tough decisions to survive by suffering silently. As a single mother, I had to decide to either fight them with my whole being or find another job that would provide me with an income that could sustain a reasonable lifestyle with some amount of peace. Legal warfare is not a peaceful existence at all.

Although I lost the appeal, I did as much as possible to advocate for myself and others. While I was not granted tenure, my case caused restructuring in the school's review process. Some policies, practices, and procedures changed due to standing up for myself. This same courage to speak my truth even when my voice shook at times is the same voice that I use in advocating for change within other spaces. I learned from that experience that there are different ways to think about change. This book is intended to help you make such impactful changes within your sphere of control and influence.

REFLECTION

What negative experiences have you had because of your identity? In what ways did you advocate for yourself personally or professionally? Was your self-advocacy more private or public? Did your self-advocacy impact others positively or negatively?

YOUR CONTEXT MATTERS

In pursuing more equitable outcomes, it is imperative to identify what you are doing and what you are hoping to do within your context. Some of you reading this book now may be in or may have filled one of the many new equity leader positions that have been created for businesses and institutions across the United States. You may understand the goal of increasing equitable outcomes in your organization, but it is likely you have encountered resistance that prevents the work from progressing. You could be a leader who does not explicitly lead equity work but must produce equitable outcomes based on the organization's vision and mission. Or you could be an employee who has participated in equity training and thought, "So, what now? What do I do with this newfound equity talk?" Or you could be someone who has suffered injustice because of who you are, and you want to think of ways to better advocate for yourself and others in similar circumstances.

My context was being assigned the role of leading equity work within my organization. I became the first equity specialist in an urban school district, and it was my dream job. It felt like the culmination of all my education experiences as a teacher, professor, and administrator who studied and advocated for marginalized people. This is where this book was born. Coming from the academy, I was used to giving students readings, having discussions, and giving assignments where we intentionally called out issues of institutional inequities, -isms, and -obias. As an academic, I became comfortable with academic freedom, which provides some protection and latitude for challenging mainstream ideas. I came into my new district administrator role like an equity tornado. After reviewing the data, I had all the challenges identified and was ready to gather everyone up to fix them. After all, they hired me for my expertise in equity. So clearly, we were about to create a more equitable environment for the students, families, and communities we served.

When I signed up to be an equity leader, I had to come to terms with the real context of where I was commissioned to do this work. Being the first-born and eldest sister in my family, I want to lead and break through barriers as best I can. As I discussed some of my initial leadership frustrations with one of my younger sisters, she replied, "Latish, Martin Luther King didn't work for no school district." She was giving me a reality check that most revolutionaries are not likely to be on the payroll in a large bureaucratic organization steeped in the status quo. Moving quickly and breaking down barriers all at once was unlikely. Changing this system would take patience and incremental work.

While I had one equity intern (who was head-and-shoulders above anything that I could have ever hoped for), I did not have a department or anyone who was specifically identified to help provide an equity lens for my district, which had over seventy thousand students and five thousand employees. Yet, the job description included writing and reviewing policies, procedures, and practices, facilitating professional development, partnering with all departments, and leading equity discussions with senior teams, management, teachers, students, and the community. When I took this role, equity officers, directors, and/or chiefs often found themselves with big orders to fill and few resources to fill them with. Nonetheless, in my setting, I found many colleagues who wanted to support this work in addition to their assigned tasks. During my time in this role, I worked to establish an equity policy, revise our nondiscrimination policy to include more gender inclusivity, and establish a district framework for culturally responsive practices.

The experiences that I had in making an impact in this organization are what led me to share how these things were accomplished. I often explain my work with the specific task of exploring and changing equity as dancing the Cha-Cha. In the Cha-Cha, couples move forward and backward with alternating fast and slow steps. But while their feet are animated and often quick in their movements, their torsos remain steady. This is how I felt many days in the work I loved. We updated and revised our nondiscrimination policy to embrace gender inclusion and provided professional development for all administrators and teachers. However, I still received calls from students and families about situations within the school where the policy was not being followed. While we passed an equity policy, the document's accompanying guidance took many years to develop.

Nonetheless, progress and impact were made during my time in this role, and I encountered many people who came to this work through different entry points. Some embraced equity, while others did not. But I always hoped that no matter how they entered, they would leave feeling more empowered and ready to change something they were doing that would lead to better outcomes for the students, families, and communities they served.

The other context for my work at that time was being the single mother of a fourth-grade Black boy who was extremely hard-working in school, had a positive disposition, and possessed all the potential in the world. This job was important for me as it was my first work experience after not being tenured. I had to pick my life up and move on. After all, I had to provide for my son, who watched his mother fight a system. I look at him today and believe that he is better for it. He will also be better for watching his mother collect her gifts and talents and move on to make new impacts in new ways and spaces. My work was about creating a better education for the thousands of children in the district and creating the right environment for my son to thrive in, so he could reach his fullest potential in that same district. The context of being a Black woman with a Black son was important for my willingness and inspiration to do as much as I could within the equity role I was serving.

THE HISTORICAL LANDSCAPE

The other critical part of identifying your context is determining the historical landscape within the organization or situation you have entered. It is important to ask yourself what you are trying to achieve given the current context. Is your organization trying to organize an initial implementation of an equity mission and vision with new policies and procedures? Has the organization been "working on equity" for a while and is now trying to understand why nothing has changed? Are you trying to understand what you specifically can do to improve the conditions within your workspace?

In my case, there had always been efforts within the school district to provide more equitable opportunities for students who were more at-risk than others due to the circumstances they were born into. That seems to be the nature of urban public education. It is tasked with educating mainly Black and Brown, economically challenged children and trying to determine ways to better serve them. There is much-needed funding allocated to what appears to be resources for improving students' educational experiences. But the question is always, "Is it enough?" Are resources being used expeditiously in a way that will improve outcomes? The measures seem clear when districts and schools set improvement goals, but there is little accountability when improvement does not occur.

I realized that it was important to illuminate the district's inequities. First, very few people in the district even understood what equity meant. After getting organized, I had to go on an organizational tour to explain "equity." That meant establishing relationships across the organization to help them to understand where inequities existed in the first place. In education, equity is often an implied goal. It is usually not codified within the organization's policies and procedures *as a need*. Once everyone understood where the inequities existed, my superintendent and chief asked me to create an equity policy and revise our nondiscrimination policy to be more gender inclusive. Again, this process included gaining insight into what equity would and should look like within the context of the district.

Part of this work included reviewing the equity frameworks, policies, and procedures in other organizations like mine. This inventory included assessing other organizations' policies, procedures, and practices. I also used the Wisconsin Response to Intervention (RtI) Center's Model to Inform Culturally Responsive Practices (2017). The framework was extremely useful in helping the district and school staff understand that there is a clinical process to becoming a more equitable individual and organization. The work of Dr. Gloria Ladson-Billing, a legendary K-12 scholar, also informed this model. The work of prolific practitioner-scholars, Drs. Anthony Muhammad and Sharroky Hollie, informed my school leadership and practical pedagogy recommendations. While this approach was intended for understanding and combating inequities within education, I have successfully adapted it to my work with government, healthcare, and corporate organizations too.

Walking into an organization as the first equity leader was a big task. However, I found it essential to understand what work had been done prior to my coming. I assembled an equity commission that represented all facets of the organization. We conducted analyses of policy, academic benchmark data, initiatives, and practices that were occurring in the district at that time. Our goal was to build upon the many positive things happening and mitigate or eradicate policies or practices that yield inequitable outcomes. If you do not carry an official title in equity, it is still important to know and understand the context and history of what you need to do to advance your team's equity outcomes. Ask yourself: How will you start the work or carry forward what has already been done meaningfully to have a positive impact?

When you think about the personal context of leading change in your life, recognize that you have been conditioned to think in specific ways about concepts such as race, class, and those with different orientations or identities. Then, you can determine how to begin. As in the professional setting, researching to determine how others think about change in these areas is a great place to start before you have conversations with the teams and groups you will work with.

There is an adage that asks, "How do you eat an elephant?" The response is "one bite at a time." As you push through "shades of gray," understand what you control, what you can influence, and the things outside of your control.

TIMING MATTERS

A Time for Everything

There is a time for everything and a season for every activity under the heavens:

> . . . a time to plant and a time to uproot, a time to kill and a time to heal, a time to tear down and a time to build . . . a time to scatter stones and a time to gather them, a time to embrace and a time to refrain from embracing, a time to search and a time to give up, a time to keep and a time to throw away, a time to tear and a time to mend, a time to be silent and a time to speak, a time to love and a time to hate, a time for war and a time for peace.
>
> Ecclesiastes 3:1-8, Bible, New International Version

The T in the ICE-T refers to the important nature of timing. In the battle for equity, windows of opportunity come and go. As someone seeking equity and justice, you will find that learning how to take advantage of timing is critical to your success. Throughout history, people have often felt injustice; however, they continued to live with it because the timing did not seem right to change it. As time passes, someone stands up to be a catalyst for changing the status quo. It may take a while for the momentum to develop. But people become engaged, the times change, and the opportunity for justice emerges.

In 1964, Dr. Martin Luther King, Jr. wrote:

> The conservatives who say, "Let us not move so fast," and the extremists who say, "Let us go out and whip the world," would tell you that they are as far apart as the poles. But there is a striking parallel: They accomplish nothing; for they do not reach the people who have a crying need to be free.

In a utopia, everyone would agree on what equity and justice look like at the same time. Unfortunately, agreement on what it appears to be and when it can be achieved is scant. Since George Floyd's death, many people who had never seriously considered injustice are trying to understand its historical and contemporary implications. A common refrain is, "I'm on a (equity) journey." On the other hand, those who have lived with injustice through their identities and experiences since coming into this world are almost always ready for change.

THE N-WORD AND BEYOND: CHANGING TERMS OVER TIME

Timing is important for so many reasons, including the use of terminology related to race. A prominent example would be the terms that I have used to describe Black people. Eligon (2020) says the "terms in America for identifying black people have evolved over generations, from colored to Negro to black and African American. Also commonly used is 'people of color,' an umbrella term used to include many ethnic minorities." Based on the era, the phrase of the day was acceptable but would turn offensive during another period.

The N-word, a racist slur, continues to draw passionate debate on who uses it and how it is used. Some individuals and organizations, like the National Association for the Advancement of Colored People (NAACP, 2014), have taken a concrete position that the term should never be used under any circumstances because of its dehumanizing history.

Others like Ta-Nehisi Coates (Random House, 2017) provide a more nuanced explanation of why some Black people still use the term. While he agrees that non-Black people should not use the N-word, he says that even with its negative connotation, some Black people use it as an insider term based on individuals' context and relationship.

In most business and professional settings, the N-word is typically not a word one would find used openly. But, in some schools, the word is used and causes race-based incidents (Anti-Defamation League, 2014). Educators who may want to teach the historical context of the word or use authentic literature but have no guidance or policies to provide safe parameters often create more harm. For the reasons cited by Coates, some Black students may use the term, confusing non-Black students about its appropriateness. In some cases, "N-word passes" are given by Black students to others, which lead to further confusion. It is essential for educators to understand how this derogatory terminology and other words associated with Black people have changed over time.

When Black people were brought to this country and enslaved, the N-word was the name given, assigned, and not permitted to dispute. During that time and today, this term is still used to denigrate Black people. During the eighteenth century, Negro was widely used. Because it was the standard convention, Fredrick Douglass, a well-known former slave and abolitionist, used the term to refer to himself and other Black people (Douglass, 2018). Starting in the nineteenth century through the mid-twentieth century, Black people were also referred to as "colored" people (Malesky, 2014). (This term is not to be confused with the contemporary phrase "people of color," which refers to all non-white people, including Black people. Currently, the term "colored people" is still considered offensive.)

However, during the Civil Rights era, many advocated to drop the terms Negro and colored and adopt the term Black. Malcolm X identified Negro as an oppressive term (Haley & Shabazz, 1989). He believed that the term Black was more empowering and instilled a needed sense of pride in Black people. Moving into the 1970s, the term Afro-American was adopted by Black people to connect their lineage to the content of Africa. In the 1980s, the term African American became popular. Eligon (2020) says that historically, Black was also a way to refer to Black people. Even today, there is a push to capitalize the B in the word Black as it describes a people and a culture. I have opted to use the capital B in this book. What we do know is that wherever we land, it could still change based on the timing and whatever is happening at that moment.

TIMESCHANGE4METOO: HOW A HASHTAG UNSILENCED WOMEN OVER TIME

The #metoo movement began when, in 2017, Gen X actress Alyss Milano urged women who had been a victim of sexual assault to use the hashtag #metoo. This action went viral, with millions of women worldwide discussing and identifying with the trauma of being sexually assaulted. What most people did not know is that a Black woman, Tarana Burke, had introduced the term eleven years earlier to give voice to Black and Brown women who had suffered silently from sexual assault. Fortunately, Milano has worked alongside Burke to amplify the resistance against sexual violence to all people in vulnerable positions. This is a prime example of how details like timing and identity can make a difference.

Another example is the case of Anita Hill, a Black intellectual who notoriously testified against conservative Justice Clarence Thomas in 1991 during his Senate Supreme Court confirmation hearings (Mock, 2013). She experienced offensive and inappropriate treatment during her testimony about the sexual harassment she experienced when Judge Thomas supervised her during her time working at the Equal Employment Opportunity Commission (EEOC). The country was riveted by Hill's live testimony in front of an all-male, all-white Senate Judiciary Committee that was combative and insensitive to her detailed account of sexual harassment inflicted by Judge Thomas. In the wake of her unplanned and unwanted notoriety, Hill became a tenured professor and remained obscure. After allowing her story to be documented in 2013, Hill shared what she had endured, noting that the timing was not right for the outrage that we see now. Women were less likely to come forth after they saw what Hill went through during and after the trials.

In her 2018 commencement speech for Wesleyan University, she admonished those in attendance by saying, "We cannot squander this moment," referring to the powerful timing of millions of voices drawing attention during the era of #metoo (MacNeill, 2019). Both Burke and Hill, two Black victims of sexual violence and harassment, remained vigilant and amplified the voice of those who suffer in silence. At the same time, Milano and numerous other white women with a broader platform used this "timing" aspect to broaden the message.

Timing was a factor in my own career when I appealed my no-tenure decision. At that time, no attorney wanted to take on my case because it was not common to challenge unfair tenure decisions. The tenure process had become highly protected over time. But in the fall of 2021, I received a call from someone at the state university's public governing board. The caller wanted to ask questions about my failed appeal because, of course, many others had come forward with similar claims of unfair and biased procedural practices. Doctoral students and other faculty had stepped forward in greater numbers after the watershed moment of George Floyd's murder. I had moved on with my life and did not want to open the past wounds by reengaging legal counsel or doing whatever was needed to seek justice. But it just showed me that sometimes, what is right may not be possible at the right time.

REFLECTION

How has the passage of time influenced the issues you are passionate about advocating for, particularly in terms of shifting societal norms or increased awareness?

Also, as an equity administrator, I was hired under a board resolution named after the Black Lives Matter movement. However, at the time, it was uncommon to say "Black Lives Matter" within the context of any school organization. The administration chose to focus more on the work called for by the resolution rather than the title of the resolution. Over time, through the grassroots efforts of some teachers and community activists, the district administration was moved to use the Black Lives

Matter at School Week to emphasize the work. The timing was better because others across the country were also holding space for Black Lives Matter within the context of education. At that point, activities were planned, and we even had a day set aside to wear BLM paraphernalia to school to celebrate the week's acknowledgment.

It is important to consider timing when moving your actions forward. There is absolutely nothing wrong with supporting and pushing unpopular actions forward in the name of justice. However, the work will be more difficult if the timing is wrong and there is not a broad understanding of the actions as necessary for equitable outcomes.

All this is complicated. And we haven't even started talking about the complexities of navigating equity. However, understanding your ICE-T (Identity, Context, Experiences, and Timing) is essential in your ability to push through the shades of gray to enact equity.

Questions to Consider

1. Describe your identity.
    a. What are "seen" or visible attributes?
    b. What are "unseen" or invisible attributes?
    c. What parts of your identity are most salient?
    d. What part of your identity do you think least about?
2. What experiences have you had because of your identity?
    a. What positive experiences have informed your feelings about advocating for yourself and others?
    b. What negative experiences have shaped your approach to advocating for yourself and others?
3. Describe the context of what you either want to do or are called to do to create more equitable outcomes.
4. Provide a timeline of the important events or context changes that have occurred in your equity work goals. How have things changed over time?

CHAPTER 2

The Equity Empowerment Continuum

A meeting at the coffee shop . . .

I received a LinkedIn message from a professional acquaintance I know from the community. She had just celebrated the one-year anniversary of her job as a DEI leader in a professional sports organization. A year prior, when I saw that she had taken on the role, I sent her a congratulatory message on LinkedIn and offered my leadership coaching services because I knew how difficult her job would be. We met at a coffee shop. It was one of my first complimentary prospecting meetings, and I quickly learned that they should be no more than 30 minutes. But before I knew it, I had been there for an hour and a half, listening to my colleague lament over how hard the work had been. At times, she was teary-eyed and visibly worn out. Hopelessness emerged as the overall conversation theme. I was filled with empathy because I shared a similar outlook as I approached my own one-year anniversary as the equity leader of a large school district.

"CALL A THING, A THING!"

The Equity Empowerment Continuum framework was born from navigating the challenges I faced as an equity leader and the subsequent years I spent in the same organization in a non-equity leadership role. I learned to "call a thing, a thing," a phrase I learned on a TV show called *Fix My Life* (Vanzant, 2012–2021). Iyanla Vanzant, a Black inspirational speaker, lawyer, spiritual teacher, author, and life coach, produced and starred in the reality show that ran from 2012 to 2021. Prospective guests contacted her show's producers with challenging relationships or situations. If accepted on the show, guests agreed to her common-sense conversations, spiritual advisement, and no-nonsense tough love. They were pushed to self-reflect before even beginning to address the real problem. When guests resisted naming the challenges they faced, she would often say, "call a thing, a thing."

Equity leaders must engage in self-reflection and use the Equity Empowerment Continuum to advance their individual and organizational equity goals. If you are serious about creating equitable change for marginalized people, you must first "call a thing a thing." You must face the truth about why this work is so hard to just "do the right thing."

With the many complex challenges that we face, it is a part of our nature to want to find the solution or tools right away. Acting before we completely understand is usually what gives us false starts and failed launches in our equity efforts. Figure 2.1 is the Equity Empowerment Continuum (EEC) framework phases. In what follows, I will explain why a continuum is an appropriate visual to explain how to classify and approach equity work.

FIGURE 2.1 • The Equity Empowerment Continuum

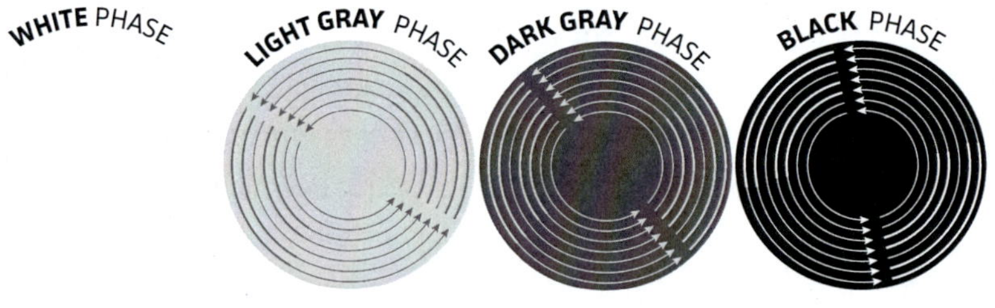

Graphic by Molly Quirk

Before explaining the Equity Empowerment Continuum (EEC), I want to describe two major barriers to equity work, internal contradictions, and the ever-present status quo gaze. Following the exploration of those two concepts, I will introduce the EEC.

THE EQUITY JOURNEY: UNRAVELING INTERNAL CONTRADICTIONS

This book acknowledges how complicated pursuing equity can be. When you think you have it, you realize you don't and, instead, need to reevaluate your perspectives and actions. This is where people seem to get most frustrated. They really want to have a clear distinction between what is right and wrong, then move always in the direction of what is right. Hopefully, as you read, you will see it is impossible to always be right and proceed without missteps, and you will understand that we must be comfortable with the process of our own evolution. As I author this book, I often ruminate about the contradictions in my own life.

One year during Black History Month, I was scrolling through the "Book of Life," also known as Facebook. I came across a clip blasting an older, famous, white male actor/comedian for saying that he missed Aunt Jemima, a fictitious house slave cook who represented a popular maple syrup brand. In June 2020, right after the watershed moment of George Floyd's murder, that company changed its brand name to Pearl Milling Company, its original name, and removed the slave cook from its logo (Haworth, 2021). The social media choir sang a loud refrain rebuking the comedian's insensitive comments. It did not occur to him that this company could and should recognize the error in glorifying slavery imagery and associating it with comfort food. I was equally appalled. And to think he had the nerve to say this during Black History Month.

A few days later, I was browsing through my TikTok timeline and came across an old Oprah Winfrey Show clip where a group of Indigenous Americans talked about the pain and challenges associated with using offensive images as mascots for sports teams. I felt completely in agreement with them until one of the women mentioned how auto companies need to change the name of certain car models. This stopped me in my tracks. The year before I had bought the truck I had wanted for many years: a Jeep Cherokee. The woman's explanation made so much sense. Why would we name a vehicle after a person or group of people, especially a group of people who had been subjected to forced relocations, and genocide? The woman even asked Oprah how she would feel if we named a car a Zulu. I got it when she turned the question into something that would feel offensive to me. Now, what do I do with this dream car sitting in my garage?

I could easily identify the insensitivity and harm caused by the comedian. However, I was privately embarrassed and ashamed that as much as I advocate for marginalized people or groups, I was completely blind to my desire to drive a car named after a group of people. If this contradiction is something I navigate personally, consider the complex contradictions and powerful feelings that must arise in the workplace, where contradictions are public and can have an adverse impact on people in the organization. In chapter 1, we discussed how identity, experience, context, and timing shape our dispositions and the equitable actions we are willing to take to change the world. The Equity Empowerment Continuum (EEC) identifies the degree to which you are willing to take risks and actions toward those equitable outcomes.

REFLECTION

What internal contradictions do you face related to your equity advocacy work? To what extent do your internal contradictions impact your work? How do you confront internal contradictions?

There are many ways to facilitate equity work. Some more mainstream more popular approaches like sensitivity training may provide a palatable entry point to discuss differences, whereas other training may provide a more critical approach that requires a disruption of the status quo. Both ends of the spectrum create progress and change. James Baldwin said, "We can disagree and still love each other unless your disagreement is rooted in my oppression and denial of my humanity and right to exist." There are various points of view and multiple ways to arrive at justice. But what do we mean by the "denial of my humanity" and the "denial of my right to exist?" To answer those questions and questions like them, the Equity Empowerment Continuum (EEC) embraces both mainstream and critical approaches to equity.

EQUITY IS UNDER THE WATCHFUL "STATUS QUO GAZE"

Before we can fully understand the EEC, we must acknowledge that it exists within the same conditions and is subject to the same difficulties that impact all equity work. Toni Morrison's unabashed explanation of the "white gaze" and how it impacts many Black authors serves as an excellent introduction to those challenges (Rose, 2015). After Morrison died in 2019, a clip from a 1998 interview with Australian journalist Jana Wendt went viral (Wendt, 2017). Wendt asked, what initially seemed to be a good-natured question, if Morrison would consider "incorporating white lives" into her books "in a substantial way." Appalled, Morrison asked Wendt if she understood how "powerfully racist" the question was. She asked if Wendt, a white woman, would ask a white writer if they planned to incorporate Black lives into their writing. As Wendt awkwardly muddled for a recovery, Morrison further explained that the question came from Wendt's "position of being in the center." Ultimately, Morrison quietly, yet passionately told Wendt that she wanted to write without the "white gaze" impacting her work.

In the 1998 documentary *Toni Morrison: The Pieces I Am,* Morrison describes to Charlie Rose how she spent her career rejecting the notion that she should write under this "white gaze" (Giebelhaus et al., 2019). But what does this mean? Morrison described that, historically, most Black authors wrote in a way that was meant to be palatable to white audiences. Notably, she refers to the works of Frederick Douglass, who partnered with white people to eliminate slavery. While these abolitionists were progressive in many ways, Douglass still censored his narrative and his demands for freedom to provide a certain comfort level for white people so that they would continue supporting and advocating for the ultimate freedom of his people. Often, people of color alter their advocacy for themselves and other people of color so as not to offend or upset white people.

Morrison was unapologetically unwilling to subscribe to this "white gaze" in her writing—the one that would diminish her soul, voice, and the stories that center Black people. She is a preeminent author, editor, and activist who ascended to inspirational heights in her career and broke many barriers (Li, 2009).

She was the first Black woman to win the Nobel Peace Prize in literature. The average person striving to make change within their organization does not have the equivalent of her celebrity or status. Yet, the average person is likely to encounter the "white gaze," or some form of it, and many other challenges to creating equity within their organization.

The EEC can help you find your voice and determine how you will act to make progress within that context. While most equity work centers on race, it also addresses issues of class, gender, gender identity, sexual orientation, (dis)ability, religious affiliation, mental wellness status, immigration status, and other marginalized identities in our society. Depending on what marginalized population you work with and belong to, you are likely to experience something like the "white gaze," which is why I also use the term "status quo gaze" to name and acknowledge the many prejudices, stereotypes, and discriminations that exist in our culture and our workplaces. The "status quo gaze" can be described as an invisible boundary that causes people to modify their actions to avoid upsetting the apple cart. For example, if you work in a place where people are mostly Christian, it may be common to discuss Christian faith or celebrations like Christmas or Easter. But it can become challenging for Muslim people in the same environment when there is no space for their faith in the workplace, and they have difficulty finding places to pray at the designated times without judgment. Jewish people may feel uncomfortable discussing their faith or celebrations in the workplace too. In most cases, people won't say anything specific about their colleagues wanting to pray at designated times or about celebrating Hanukkah, but it is often clear to those of Jewish and Muslim faiths that their actions and conversations make those from the majority religion uncomfortable.

REFLECTION

How does the "status quo gaze" impact your work setting? How do individuals maintain the status quo to avoid the "status quo gaze?"

When organizations commit to equity efforts on paper, the "status quo gaze" looms over their efforts and the efforts of those engaged in the work. They encounter seen and unseen barriers to equity. Most barriers are invisible. Consequently, I often felt like I was walking on eggshells while doing this work. There were times when I wanted to maintain a healthy work relationship with my colleagues. I also wanted to sustain a personal work-life balance with boundaries that allowed me to detach from work challenges. However, challenging the status quo nearly always involves making someone uncomfortable. I sometimes feared that if I made the wrong person with organizational power and control uncomfortable, it might lead to a shutdown of the entire equity program. For similar reasons, equity professionals constantly struggle with self-censorship about what they say and do. This debilitating burden privileges the status quo and those who benefit from it instead of the minoritized individuals most in need of equitable change.

INTRODUCING THE EQUITY EMPOWERMENT CONTINUUM

Before I introduce the EEC, I want to acknowledge one of its quirks. Critiques of this book may call the EEC a way to water down equity work. The pursuit of "life, liberty, and happiness" has been a part of the rhetorical fabric of the US since its inception and at least the Declaration of Independence. When the country was founded, women and Black people were not considered worthy of those lofty declarations. Over time, the national vision has expanded to include them. That long path to justice is reflected in a chant that can be heard at any modern-day protest: "What do we want? JUSTICE!!! When do we want it? NOW!!!" We do not want to believe that equitable actions take time, that they require a process that must be carefully navigated. This is a common thread in my work.

As an equity leader, I have interfaced with various community members, teachers, students, a progressive school board of directors, and union members. They have all questioned the pace at which their equity work was codified and implemented. While my work was ultimately well-received, I also received feedback that the work was going too slowly. Many times, the messages about equity that I delivered and endorsed did not seem to match the results. What observers did not understand was that my work required strategic thinking and planning over a long period of time.

The EEC is a tool that helps you think about what you will do and how. It is a framework that unpacks and analyzes the opportunities at hand for making meaningful progress. It will help you see where you are in your equity work and where you want to go, and it will help us consider the steps necessary for empowering more impactful actions.

When I began my doctoral program at the University of Wisconsin-Madison, I became immersed in social justice leadership ideology. Social justice seemed to be a mechanism for fighting against the discomfort I have described and the many barriers, visible and invisible, that prevent justice for marginalized individuals and groups. While my specific area of interest was pursuing equity within the educational realm, I quickly realized that education was only the beginning. Equitable decision-making applies in all areas where change and justice are needed. This framework is not just for large organizations but also individuals because while policies provide the opportunity for change, people need to enact it.

What does this mean? We have numerous laws and policies that supposedly stop discrimination, yet through the advent of social media, we see that discrimination persists. We have workplace policies meant to equalize hiring opportunities, yet inequality persists. We have the Americans with Disabilities Act, but people with special needs continue to need advocates. We have laws that make it unconstitutional to limit any group's ability to vote, yet we still need contemporary federal legislation to make voting more accessible to all US citizens. Why? Because people continue to use the status quo as a sphere of control and influence to perpetuate actions or inactions that lead to inequities.

Despite the numerous challenges associated with moving the equity needle, you must ground yourself in what you can and will do to that end. Policies and programs do not change practice, but people do. The EEC is a way to visualize various shades representing the degree to which you and/or your organization are willing to move on an equity issue and/or agenda. Discussing and analyzing inequity is a good place to start, but the actions you take to provide equity are what will make a difference. My mother used to say, "More of the same produces no change." In other words, you must choose to do something different to get different results.

The EEC was inspired by Dr. Martin Luther King, Jr.'s description of the arc of the moral universe. On March 25, 1965, at the end of the march from Selma to the state capital, Dr. King delivered a speech on the steps of the Alabama State Capitol in Montgomery. Before this speech, demonstrators had organized to peacefully protest the recent police killing of a man named Jimmie Lee and the segregationist attacks on the voting rights of Black men and women across the American South. The protesters were led by Rev. Hosea Williams of the Southern Christian Leadership Conference (SCLC) and Congressmen John Lewis, who was serving as the chairman of the Student Nonviolent Coordinating Committee (SNCC). The protests were met with police violence. One of the days was infamously dubbed "Bloody Sunday" because so many were injured and had to be taken to the hospital. These horrific scenes were captured and televised, which caused national outrage. As a result, President Lyndon B. Johnson sent the National Guard to ensure the safety of the protesters.

In the culminating speech that Dr. King delivered once the protestors had made it safely to the capitol steps, he discussed the many challenges they had encountered. He also affirmed that progress had been made. In his penultimate cry for truth, he declares "The arc of the moral universe is long, but it bends towards justice." Even though their goals had not been fully actualized that day, the protestor's sacrifice had moved them all closer to the goal of equality.

Over time, this statement has been critiqued, criticized, and politicized. Some believe these words were too tempered and not radical enough. On the other hand, overt and covert threats to Black lives were real during that time. Dr. King's life was in a constant state of threat. His life and the lives of many others ended at the hands of assassins who felt threatened by the promise of racial justice. Those who choose to speak up for change today are also regularly targeted and attacked. Similarly, many people within educational and professional organizations, or even people trying to shift their mindset from harmful ways of thinking, receive threats that impact their lives in negative ways.

The EEC is a way to recognize and navigate the real threats that exist within your context. When you can see and consider where you are on the continuum, you can begin to bend "the arc" closer to justice. It usually does not happen as swiftly and certainly as we would like. As a Black woman in America, I think of my ancestors, most of whom remain nameless to me. I am sure they never envisioned a descendant who was free from the kind of slavery they lived with, who has a terminal degree in education, an administration job with healthcare, and a promised retirement plan. Whenever my enslaved ancestors arrived in this country, the arc of the moral universe was long and bent toward justice. Today, I may be free on paper, but I still experience oppression and marginalization, and so the bending continues.

Table 2.1 provides descriptions of each phase in the EEC, which will be further detailed in the following four chapters. Identifiers and outcomes are also provided for consideration.

TABLE 2.1 • EEC Descriptions, Identifiers, and Outcomes

WHITE	LIGHT GRAY	DARK GRAY	BLACK
Absence of action or actively deepening inequities **Identifiers:** • Avoidance • Misinformation • Dialing back progress **Outcome:** Deepened inequities	Superficial or performative actions that mildly address inequities **Identifiers:** • Performative Allyship • Kicking can down the road • No money where your mouth is **Outcome:** More of the same	Pushing the boundaries within the organization to create equitable changes **Identifiers:** • Maximizing your networks • Using your ICE-T to create Win-Wins • Create Written Accountability **Outcome:** Progress	Large-scale laws of the land that provide the foundation for equity work **Identifiers:** • Aspiration to Action • Symbols and Movements • Comprehensive Codification **Outcome:** Toward Justice

In the Equity Empowerment Continuum, equity exists in varying degrees. How and to what degree we enact equitable actions are likely attached to how strongly we feel about an injustice we are charged to address. We are often moved to action by events or causes that impact our lives directly. But when others need an advocate, you may not be able to embrace the struggle and move forward.

BEYOND BOUNDARIES: EXPANDING THE SCOPE OF YOUR EQUITY WORK

One of my favorite quotes from Dr. Martin Luther King's "Letter from a Birmingham Jail" is: "An injustice anywhere is a threat to justice everywhere. We are caught in an inescapable network of mutuality, tied in a single garment of destiny. Whatever affects one directly affects all indirectly." This message urges us to advocate beyond our immediate causes and embrace equity for all. During my doctoral program, I extended my advocacy reach. As a Black woman, I spent most of my career working in schools with mostly Black children. I was passionate about providing them with equitable opportunities and support to them. While at the University of Wisconsin-Madison, under the guidance of Dr. Colleen Capper, I realized that I had overlooked the specific needs of LGBTQIA+ students. This realization moved me to learn how to serve all students, regardless of their identities or identity intersections.

As the new district equity leader, I was immediately confronted with questions related to gender inclusion. Transgender students in the district received inconsistent support navigating their school context. Using what I learned in graduate school, I moved forward to provide support for students by leading a revision to our nondiscrimination policy and the development of comprehensive guidance for the staff. While we faced resistance, these steps marked progress in our commitment to equity. Pushing through the shades of gray requires us to go beyond the issues and causes we are comfortable with to expand our advocacy reach.

I choose to use black, white, and shades of gray to describe the equity continuum because black and white are two colors that provide a clear binary. In 2022, I turned fifty years old. It has been a great experience to reflect upon my life at the half-century milestone. When I was an undergraduate, my sorority sister said, "Latish sees things as either black or white; for her, there really isn't any gray area." Those words stuck with me for many years. As I navigated my life, I realized what she meant. I am the kind of person who does something wholeheartedly. Until recent years, in most situations, I stood fast to what I believed. Approaching my milestone birthday and reflecting upon my career in education, I realized that life has been filled with many shades of gray. Within the EEC, light and dark gray capture actions that may lead to progress or change, but to varying degrees. This complexity will unfold in the next four chapters.

Questions to Consider

1. In what ways do you reflect on your self-awareness of equity topics?
2. What internal contradictions do you have that may impact your ability to advocate for equity?
3. Discuss the concept of the "status quo gaze" and its impact on equity work within your organizations.
4. How do you balance the interests of those with different perspectives on addressing equity in your work setting?

CHAPTER 3

The White Phase

To begin, I will describe what white symbolizes in the context of the Equity Empowerment Continuum (EEC). Encyclopedia Britannica (2024) defines white from a physics perspective, indicating it is "light the human eye can see when all visible spectrum wavelengths combine." In other words, it is a combination of all colors, though it is also the lightest. But, from an artistic and perceptual perspective, white is perceived as "the absence of color" because it reflects all colors at once. Given this common experience, white symbolizes the absence of action in the EEC.

I do realize that associating the color white with something negative may cause discomfort. But remember, the previous description of the color white does not refer to people; it refers to a scientific and artistic understanding of the perception of light and color and therefore denotes its absence. Associating the EEC's definition of white with a race of people can invoke "white fragility" (DiAngelo, 2018). But in the EEC, the categories that follow white are light gray and dark gray. Gray is not a race, nor is white in this case, and the first phase in this conceptual framework is not intended to be associated with skin color.

In the EEC, the White Phase is categorized by avoidance, providing misinformation, and dialing back progress. These (in)actions are harmful to equity work and progress. They prevent support and/or resources from reaching marginalized people and communities. In what follows, these categories are explained and illustrated with contextualized general and education-specific examples to clarify each concept.

AVOIDANCE

Avoidance occurs when people or organizations refuse to address challenges related to inequities. It reminds me of being "married to mediocrity." This is a comfortable space where, just like in a bad marriage, it becomes easier to stay in an unhealthy relationship than to get the counseling help needed to improve the relationship or make the tough decision to separate. We avoid addressing certain issues because we fear backlash from those who oppose the change. Furthermore, the change may spark discomfort within us.

"ICK-QUITY" CAUSES AVOIDANCE

On a personal and professional level, individuals may fully understand the inequities in their communities, workplaces, country, and world. However, that may not be enough to compel them to action. The first identifier of white action is avoidance because addressing the challenges creates discomfort that people are unwilling to accept. I work hard to create a space where people can engage authentically in the equitable and culturally responsive sessions I facilitate. While working to address serious issues, I also sometimes use humor to disarm my audience. Once, in an equity training I was leading, I attempted to say that "it gets icky when we start talking about equity." But "icky" came out as "ICK-quity." Everyone in the room stopped and laughed uncomfortably, but we all understood exactly what I meant. ICK-quity is the uncomfortable feeling that people have when trying to discuss or address issues that deal with inequitable, culturally insensitive behavior, discrimination, or injustice.

In many of my professional development sessions, I show a video of Dr. Alexis McGill Johnson, who describes how discussions of implicit bias can trigger anxiety (Johnson, 2015). She specifically discusses racial anxiety from the perspective of how people feel when "race [or any other marginalized topic] drops into the conversation." She says that if you are white (or in a majority group), you may be fearful that you will be seen as operating out of racism (or any other -ism or phobia). If you are a person of color or another marginalized group, she proposes that you may become worried, that you may be invalidated, and that you may not be seen fairly or truthfully by others. She explains that our executive brain goes into fight or flight mode when this anxiety arises. In one group where I shared this clip, one participant added that we may also freeze and fall into an eerie silence. These responses garner emotional and physical reactions and lead us to work hard to protect ourselves from feeling ICK-quity.

REFLECTION

Have you ever been in a conversation where it became "ICK-quity" because of a sensitive topic like race, gender identity, religion, class, language, or immigration status that felt uncomfortable? Was there a "fight or flight" response, and could participants work through it to reach a productive resolution or understanding? What did that process look like?

A classic example of avoidance is not acknowledging and addressing the deep wealth and poverty inequities in the US. Writing for the Pew Research Center, Horowitz et al. (2020) explain that despite recent gains in the US economy, "economic inequality, whether measured through the gaps in income or wealth between richer and poorer households" has continued to widen, a trend that began in the 1970s.

Solutions to mitigating poverty through alternative tax strategies have been proposed by many economists, politicians, and scholars. In a 2023 NPR interview, host Dave Davies (2023) spoke with the Princeton sociologist and Pulitzer Prize-winning author of *Evicted*, Mathew Desmond, who described how the wealthy often benefit more from tax breaks than the poor. He explained that "most government aid goes to families that need it the least" and remarked that after adding up tax breaks that include "mortgage interest deduction, wealth transfer tax breaks, tax breaks we get on our retirement accounts, our health insurance, our college savings accounts—you learn that we are doing so much more to subsidize affluence than to alleviate poverty." While we may know exactly what needs to be done to fix this crisis, we do not change it. We avoid it, both privately and publicly.

Similarly, we understand inequity in schools very well. We know some things need to change, but we avoid changing them due to the anticipated backlash and discomfort. Whether you are a named equity leader or someone who wants to lead with an equity lens, you understand that making substantial organizational changes is daunting. Those coming into the work will recognize that many prefer to remain comfortable and operate within the status quo rather than make difficult decisions. Hence, many often choose not to address inequities within their organization. However, avoidance keeps the organization stagnant and creates a culture of ongoing oppression and marginalization. In what follows, I will illustrate how avoidance can impede equity progress in the educational environment. When you know there is injustice and fail to act, you allow injustice to continue.

AVOIDANCE IN PRACTICE: A COURAGEOUS CONVERSATION GONE BAD

After leaving my district equity leader position and moving into another department, I learned firsthand why individuals can fall into avoidance even when they want to address unfair conditions or circumstances at work. The role of this department was to support new teachers. About 90 percent of the teachers we served were teachers of color. We had an upcoming series of after-school orientations planned for them. Even though the event was quickly approaching, our immediate supervisor did not communicate a plan for the orientation. A few of the staff members made some suggestions to ensure that the event went smoothly. However, our supervisor did not receive or incorporate the suggestions into the process. On the day of the event, the staff was unclear and confused.

During the after-school program orientation in August, the teachers were to line up to collect their materials. It is important to note that most of the schools in the district do not have air conditioning, so many of the teachers have been on their feet all day in the hot weather working with students. The process was also confusing and slow for the teachers because the staff was unclear due to not receiving a plan from the supervisor. To get materials, each teacher had to stop and check in with the program supervisor, who was white, and then make their way through a line to pick up materials from the remaining staff, who happened to be all Black. I was frustrated as I watched these teachers wait and stand in line without chairs or water.

I planned to bring this problem up before the next staff meeting. I wanted to use the Courageous Conversations About Race (Singleton, 2014) protocol that we had all been trained to use. One part of this protocol requires that people share their experiences using a compass, acknowledging that everyone comes to conversations about race differently. Entry points include how one believes, acts, feels, or thinks. The protocol calls for individuals to recognize "multiple perspectives." Those interested in having an authentic, courageous conversation also must isolate their race by identifying it as it provides context for everyone's experience.

Everyone seemed to be on board with having the conversation within this framework. As I began to share my perspectives as a Black woman (isolating race), I talked about feeling very anxious (my compass perspective) as I watched exhausted Black and brown teachers wait to receive materials in a single file line when we could have made the process smoother and more expedient for them. I said it reminded me of a welfare line. The conversation quickly fell off the rails. The supervisor became very defensive and discounted my perspective. She kept reiterating that she did not see this situation the same way. No one else said anything, and the conversation was drawn to a quick halt. Unfortunately, the process remained in place for subsequent material pick-up times.

Our working environment became extremely "ICK-quity." Analyzing what I saw as a racialized problem using a conversation protocol sounded like a promising idea on the front end. But it ruffled the wrong people's feathers, resulting in a negative work culture and climate for me. In that instance, it became clear why most people say nothing when they see something wrong. In this case, my supervisor avoided addressing a problem brought to her. Not only did nothing change, but work became extremely uncomfortable for my co-workers as well. In real life, most people want to avoid working in a tense environment and will do anything they can to avoid it and follow the course of least resistance.

MISINFORMATION

One of the most detrimental white identifiers is the spread of misinformation, which multiplies and worsens inequities. For example, the AIDS epidemic was a momentous time in US history where misinformation led to avoidance with catastrophic results. I remember being in the sixth grade when I first heard about AIDS. The disease sounded so scary. In my eleven-year-old mind, it seemed that neither I nor any of my family members could get it because it was said that the disease only affected gay men. I would not classify my home as homophobic, but we were not raised to be accepting of "that lifestyle." At the time, I did not realize that calling the life of a gay person "a lifestyle" was a homophobic slur and a way to "other" people. The expectation was that my sisters and I were all "straight" and would marry straight men one day as adults. So, the fact that early reports classified AIDS as a disease that exclusively impacted promiscuous gay men signaled to me that there was no way I could get this horrific disease.

According to HIV.gov, it is true that 70 percent of new HIV cases in 2021 were reported as involving gay, bisexual, or men who reported male-to-male sexual contact. However, 22 percent of new HIV cases were women and 40 percent of new HIV cases occurred in Black patients, though only 12 percent of the US population is Black. So, in all actuality, as a Black woman who identifies as cisgender and heterosexual, I am at greater risk for this incurable disease than many others. Misinformation about HIV and AIDS is still a challenge today and articles are still written to dispel long-held myths about the disease.

I was in middle school in 1984 when the story of Ryan White broke. Ryan was about my age and had been diagnosed with AIDS (Health Resources & Services Administration, n.d.). He contracted the disease through a blood transfusion he received as part of hemophilia treatments. This news story flipped my understanding of AIDS transmission on its head because this was not one of the ways transmittal had been described in the media. Now, just as gay men had been demonized, the country watched Ryan be marginalized, mistreated, and discriminated against because of his diagnosis.

Initially, it was reported that you could get HIV by kissing or hugging someone with the disease, which was untrue. After many years, a concerted effort was made to provide correct information to the public so that people understood they could not contract the disease from normal, everyday contact. Unfortunately, Ryan was driven out of his home and forced to move to a community that accepted him (Health Resources & Services Administration, n.d.).

The Centers for Disease Control and Prevention first learned about AIDS in 1981 (Reagan's Response, n.d.). However, President Ronald Reagan did not publicly address the crisis until asked about it in a press conference in 1985. He first discussed it formally in a 1987 speech close to the end of his second term in office.

There were 100,777 deaths reported to the CDC between 1981 and 1990 due to HIV and AIDS (Centers for Disease Control and Prevention, 1991). Over time, we learned more about HIV and AIDS. Even so, many lost their lives due to misinformation and failure to address this devastating epidemic that was spread and left uncorrected for many years. Today, the Centers for Disease Control and Prevention and the National Institutes of Health consistently publish awareness articles to debunk the misinformation from the early years. How many lives could have been saved if the powers had properly informed people about the disease?

CRT: CULTURALLY RESPONSIVE TEACHING OR CRITICAL RACE THEORY?

After seven years as an assistant professor, I returned to K-12 practice to work in a district as the inaugural equity administrator. I began working with two outstanding culturally responsive teacher leaders. They had been working to infuse culturally responsive teaching practices (which I will call CRT1) within a diverse district that served approximately 80 percent of students of color, students speaking over forty languages, several immigrant families, students with various religious affiliations, students with special needs, students with needs related to gender identity, and students with various sexual orientations and identities. I often met with the two teacher leaders to flesh out what providing equity would look like across the district. Our vision included embracing culturally responsive teaching (CRT1). They always used the acronym CRT to describe their work. I kept quiet at first because I was completely confused by how they infused Critical Race Theory (which I will call CRT2) into their professional development. Finally, one day, I asked why they were using Critical Race Theory because it is dense for school-aged students and confusing for most people outside the academy. We all laughed when they explained they were using CRT to refer to culturally responsive teaching.

These two passionate educators were advocating for the works of scholars like Dr. Gloria Ladson-Billings to be brought to life in schools. Her culturally responsive pedagogy was one that I was familiar with as I had taken her course as a doctoral student while at the University of Wisconsin–Madison. Culturally Responsive Teaching is a perspective or mindset that centers students and their needs, particularly those with more marginalized identities. In the case of Ladson-Billings (1995, 2014), three tenets define culturally relevant pedagogy: academic success, cultural competence, and critical consciousness.

Academic Success means that educators create opportunities for students to demonstrate success. They hold high expectations for their students regardless of their identities or contexts. *Cultural Competence* means that educators build relationships with students to understand their perspectives while bringing that context and content into the classroom for students to relate to and build upon. Finally, *Critical Consciousness* connects education to the real world. Teaching students to be critical about even their education encourages them to question what creates inequities and oppression in communities.

When I became the district equity administrator, I was fresh from the academy, where I had been immersed in supporting administrative leadership candidates through scholarship and practical knowledge. Many in the academy used Critical Race Theory (CRT2) to explain the why inequities exist within our educational system. Most scholars that write about CRT2 are not concerned with K-12 textbooks or even K-12 education. The audience is typically graduate-level students writing master's theses and dissertations that require conceptual and empirical frameworks to support them. Nothing in any class I took spoke directly to teaching Critical Race Theory (CRT2) in schools. Culturally Responsive Teaching (CRT1) advocates for students to be taught about themselves and to look at the world through a critical lens.

WHAT CRITICAL RACE THEORY IS

In the current climate, CRT2 in education has been misconstrued and inflated to become a political football. When asked what CRT2 is, most people outside of education need help to articulate it. Sawchuk (2021) says that CRT2 originated from various academic fields, including sociology and literary theory, examining the connection between political power, social organization, and language. It has influenced fields like humanities, social sciences, and education. Despite its theoretical origins, CRT2 is now often incorrectly cited as the basis for diversity and inclusion efforts.

George (2020) summarizes that Critical Race Theory (CRT2) evolved from Critical Legal Studies (CLS), which challenged the idea of law being objective or apolitical. While CLS marked a departure from earlier views of law as neutral, CRT2 went further by highlighting how the law perpetuates racial inequality. Unlike CLS, CRT2 scholars acknowledged that law could reinforce and challenge social injustice. They recognized the potential for the law to uphold civil rights and promote racial equality, diverging from the approach of destabilizing the legal system that was advocated for by some scholars.

There are disagreements about how to address injustices emphasized by CRT2, such as racially segregated schools and the disproportionate discipline of Black students. CRT2 is distinct from culturally relevant teaching but aims to help students identify and critique the causes of social inequality. Misrepresentations of CRT2 in schools have fueled debates, with critics fearing the perpetuation of what they see as damaging ideas. However, CRT2 scholarship is rarely if ever found in curricula.

New legislation targeting CRT2 is vague and potentially unconstitutional. Texas and Florida have been in the spotlight for their legislative CRT2-related bans. Reilly (2022) of *Time Magazine* notes that the Texas bill mandates that teachers do not have to teach current events. If they choose to teach current events, they must do so in an "unbiased way." However, it does not define what "unbiased" means. The Florida legislature passed the "Stop WOKE" Act (Stop the Wrongs to Our Kids and Employees Act [Stop WOKE], 2022). This law prohibits explicitly teaching that people and systems are inherently oppressive against any identity group regardless of the factual history that supports it. The law considers such training or professional conduct discriminatory. Additionally, parents, most of whom are not formally trained in education, can review and name anything in the curriculum that causes them "discomfort." This law leaves educators unclear on what would make anyone uncomfortable, resulting in speculation.

The debate over CRT2 echoes historical concerns about exposing students to certain ideas, such as socialism and Marxism in the mid-twentieth century.

MISINFORMATION ABOUT CRT2

In a podcast with host Anderson (2013–Present), Professor Emerita Gloria Ladson-Billings, one of the key scholars who used critical race theory to analyze education, shared her perspectives about CRT2 and how it is framed in the current political climate. She expresses concerns about the widespread misunderstanding and misapplication of CRT2 in education and she observes that CRT2 has been wrongly used as a catch-all term for discussions on diversity, equity, and unrelated topics like LGBTQIA issues and social-emotional learning. She then emphasizes that CRT2 is not synonymous with any conversation about race and education; it is a specific theoretical framework with distinct principles and concepts. At one point, she remarks, "It is fascinating to me how the term has been literally sucked of all of its meaning and has now become 'anything I don't like.'"

She highlights the misidentification of the "1619 Project" by Hannah-Jones (2021) as CRT2, clarifying that it is a journalistic endeavor to explore the historical significance of 1619, not a theoretical application of CRT2. Moreover, Hannah-Jones is the sole author of the "1619 Project." Ladson-Billings criticizes the tendency to dismiss discussions about race in the classroom, often justified by concerns about making white children uncomfortable. She challenges this notion by recalling her own experiences as a student reading racially charged literature without consideration for her feelings. She recalls:

> I had to sit there in a mostly white classroom in Philadelphia and read *Huckleberry Finn,* with Mark Twain with a very liberal use of the n-word. And most of my classmates just snickering. I'd take it. I'd read it. It didn't make me feel good. I had to read Robinson Crusoe. I had to read Margaret Mitchell's *Gone with the Wind*. I had to read *Heart Of Darkness*. All of these books which we have canonized are books of their time. And they often make us feel a particular kind of way about who we are in this society. But all of a sudden, one group is protected. We can't let white children feel bad about what they read.

Ladson-Billings argues that education should not solely focus on workforce preparation but also on fostering critical thinking skills, civic engagement, and healthy debate. She laments the difficulty of engaging in meaningful discussions about CRT2 when many participants lack a basic understanding of the theory. She suggests that some opposition to CRT2 may be fueled by political agendas rather than genuine concern for education and equity.

Such misinformation has caused a lot of confusion and fear for educators because the potential for labeling something as CRT2 depends largely on how opponents to equity work see it and not on the merits of the equity work itself. As a result, both educational leaders and teachers are afraid to raise historical facts about oppression and marginalization for fear of being disciplined or, even worse, fired from their jobs. This leads us naturally to the next white identifier.

REFLECTION

How has misinformation about Critical Race Theory affected the equity work in your setting? How have discussions around being culturally responsive to the communities you serve been handled in your workplace?

DIALING BACK EQUITY PROGRESS

Dialing back equity progress refers to deconstructing or removing advancements that increase equal and equitable outcomes for marginalized people. Efforts to advocate for oppressed people and groups have always been underway. Abolitionists fought to do away with slavery. Women suffragists sought to secure women the right to vote. Social advocates pursued laws to protect those with disabilities. The LGBTQIA community fought for marriage equality. And the list goes on. The efforts mentioned above all succeeded in establishing new laws or policies that led to advancements for oppressed people or groups. Black slaves were freed. Women won the right to vote. The Americans with Disabilities Act continues to protect people with disabilities in public places, workplaces, and schools. Same-sex couples' right to marriage is now protected under federal law.

In this book's introduction, I outlined the ebbs and flows of DEI work. After George Floyd's murder, there was a surge in human capital and resources dedicated to more carefully educating and examining institutions and workplaces for inequities. However, the tide has changed, and there is a coordinated effort to stop this progress with the similar legislation listed in this chapter. In the K-12 sector, teachers have been limited in their ability to teach curriculum in their expertise related to topics like race and gender identity. Additionally, funding for key positions and departments has been reduced. In business, DEI positions, teams, and initiatives have also been cut, decreasing messages of inclusiveness and slowing efforts to diversify the workforce (Creary, 2024). Topics like racial and gender equality are avoided in training. In higher education, many programs created to help marginalized students feel welcomed and comfortable on campuses have been eliminated, causing students to feel isolated (Parker, 2023).

Of course, both avoidance and the spread of misinformation can impact how efforts for equality and equity are undermined for marginalized people or groups. But in some cases, rolling back advancements is an intentional action connected to political power, control, and influence. Just as advocacy to bring about change was strategically coordinated, intentionally scaling back these efforts can be a long-term strategic process.

DIALING BACK A WOMAN'S RIGHT TO CHOOSE

In 1973, the monumental *Roe v. Wade* (1973) Supreme Court decision was rendered. As a fifty-plus-year-old woman, I had only known reproductive freedom rights over my body until 2022. President Donald Trump was able to nominate and confirm three conservative-leaning judges to the Supreme Court during his presidency, making the court a 6-3 conservative majority. After that, the Supreme Court became less likely to rule in favor of progressive measures even though Justices are supposed to judge impartially. The post-Trump Court's interpretation of the Constitution has deemed equitable progress unconstitutional, thus dialing back equity progress. For example, in 2022, after fifty years, *Roe v. Wade* was reversed, which means that women in the US are not guaranteed choice and control over their bodies where childbirth is concerned. McCann et al. (2024) of *The New York Times* reported that twenty-one states now ban abortion or restrict the procedure earlier in pregnancy than the standard set by *Roe v. Wade*.

While the impact of this decision has yet to be fully understood, the early data demonstrates that this dialing back could hurt women in their midlife. Between the ages of forty and sixty-five, women often experience a reduction in attention to reproductive needs as fertility wanes. As a result, some women who do not wish to become mothers in their later years experience unintended pregnancies and, depending on the state in which they reside, may not have access to the medical care they want. It could even impact the medical care they receive during pregnancy (Berg & Woods, 2023).

Further, abortion restrictions disproportionately affect poor women and women of color due to systemic racism and economic limitations (Bose, 2022). Black women are more likely to be concentrated in states with abortion bans, creating a condition for them to likely be criminalized for obtaining the procedure. To illustrate, in Mississippi, where bans are enacted, Black women comprise 38 percent of the population, while nationally, Black women make up only 13 percent of the US population. Limited resources and transportation options make accessing abortion services difficult (Hassanein, 2022).

DIALING BACK ACCESS TO HIGHER EDUCATION

We have witnessed the dialing back of important advancements in educational access for people of color too. On July 4, 2026, the US will be two hundred fifty years old. Over time, our country has struggled with educating people of color, especially Black people. It was only in 1950 that public universities were desegregated (*Sweatt v. Painter*, 1950). Recognizing grave imbalances in how people of color and women accessed education, measures were taken to provide equity and access through affirmative action. In 2023, these efforts were scaled back and reversed when the US Supreme Court struck down Affirmative Action and thus consideration of race in higher education admissions.

Countless people worked hard, strategized, fought, and lost their lives in pursuit of education for Black people in the US. Historically, the US waged a concerted effort to keep enslaved people uneducated. After a major slave uprising in 1739, enslaved Black people in the US were prohibited from education in states such as Alabama, Georgia, and Missouri (Maddox, 2022). Wesson (2022) notes that if slaves were caught reading or writing, they could be beaten. If white people were caught teaching enslaved individuals, they were sanctioned with excessive fines. If they were caught a second time, they could be sentenced to death. The Black community developed a complex, underground system of education where they outsmarted white enslavers and tricked them into thinking they were learning trades. In actuality, they were learning how to read and write. Literacy was a powerful tool for freedom. If enslaved individuals knew how to write, they could create passes to allow other enslaved people to escape to the North, not to mention the freedom that comes with the exploration of mental freedom.

The Harvard Education Library documents that after the Civil War, legislative efforts were made to provide public education to freed slaves in the South. Even still, Black anti-literacy efforts continued through the Jim Crow era as evidenced in *Sweatt v. Painter* (1950) and *Brown v. Board of Education* (1954), which declared "separate, but equal" unconstitutional and desegregated public universities and schools.

In 1961, President John Kennedy implemented the first executive order to bring access parity to federal contractors. Executive Order 10925 requires contractors to take "affirmative action to ensure that applicants are treated equally without regard to race, color, religion or national origin." President Lyndon Johnson extended this affirmation in The Civil Rights Act of 1964, which disallowed employment discrimination by large employers. Following these landmark actions, a series of protections were implemented to monitor discrimination based on race. The Equal Employment Opportunity Commission (EEOC) was established as a major compliance entity. Under the Nixon Administration, gender and disability were added to the protections granted by affirmative action.

These executive actions taken by those three presidents sought to decrease discrimination and increase access to college admissions for people of color and women. However, these significant efforts came with challenges. Court cases like Regents of the *University of California v. Bakke* (1978) and *Fisher v. University of Texas at Austin* (2016) reshaped college admissions, allowing race to be a factor but banning quotas.

Ultimately, on June 29, 2023, the US Supreme Court ruled on the *Students for Fair Admissions v. Harvard College* (2023) and *Students for Fair Admission v. University of North Carolina* (2023) cases that the two universities, private and public, respectively, had violated the Fourteenth Amendment of the US Constitution and Title VI of the Civil Rights Act of 1964 ("Title VI") by considering race in their admissions processes. This ruling was a major blow to ensuring equal access to people of color in this country. While only seventy-five years have passed since universities were technically desegregated, now there is little assurance that people of color will have fair access to them.

Dialing back progress is happening in both higher and K-12 education. The recent outcomes will have a lasting impact for years to come. We will study the impact of this decision on college admissions for people of color. It will take years to reduce the conservative judicial leaning of the US Supreme Court. Reinstating race-based consideration as constitutional can happen only after several years of complex political strategy that would yield the kind of justices that could change this ruling.

Similarly, as discussed in the previous section, for K-12, many laws have been created to stop teachers from teaching a more balanced curriculum that includes different perspectives and provides sufficient context information to allow students to become more critical thinkers about past challenges. Groups like Moms for Liberty continue to lobby for state legislation restricting equity-minded and culturally responsive teaching. The impact has led to educators avoiding teaching anything under scrutiny (GLAAD, 2024).

REFLECTION

How does the status of issues like women's reproductive rights or affirmative action initiatives affect your ability to serve your students or clients?

In sum, avoidance, providing misinformation, and dialing back progress leads to stalled attempts for a more equitable environment. Those engaging in these actions and behaviors are intentional about their desired outcomes. But, for those who ascribe to be equity advocates or leaders, you must identify when these behaviors are happening. Understanding that opposition and resistance is crucial to navigating the restrictions.

END-OF-CHAPTER CONSIDERATIONS: BEST PRACTICES GONE BAD

Mr. Jamar Jones is a Black principal in a metropolitan school district that has been deemed in need of improvement (INOI) for the past ten years. Mr. Jones's ICE-T is that he is a young Black male who has been in education for fifteen years. He almost did not make it to college. Still, through the support of his family and educators at his high school, he applied and enrolled at a prestigious college where he received a full academic scholarship and majored in education. He taught and served as an assistant principal at predominantly Black and Brown schools impacted by poverty in low-income areas. Five years ago, the district realized that the student population of its flagship magnet school was increasingly becoming more Black and Brown. While the increase in diversity was a positive step towards equity and access, many teachers could not adjust to the shift. While the students of color at the school demonstrated potential for success, their achievements were not reflected in grades and standardized test scores.

Although there had never been a Black principal, Mr. Jones was encouraged to apply to help ensure success with the increased number of students of color. After several interviews with the staff, community, and superintendent, the time was right, and Mr. Jones became the prestigious school's first Black male principal. After five years, Mr. Jones became somewhat of a "golden child" because he successfully led his staff to improve outcomes. It also helps that Mr. Jones had a charismatic personality. He typically had a good rapport with his directors, chiefs, colleagues, and the superintendent, and he was well-respected by his staff, students, and families.

The State Department of Public Instruction asked the district to create a strategic plan using central service personnel and school-level principals who showed positive outcomes in academic and behavioral data. Because the district had the INOI designation, the state had committed to releasing significant additional funding streams to support professional development and purchasing new technology for the district. The funds were intended to help schools with the most academic needs.

Because of the improvement at his school over the previous five years, Mr. Jones was asked to be on this team. The charge was to identify five key district goals and develop district and school-level strategies to address them. Mr. Jones was so excited to serve in this capacity because he believed he would have the opportunity to share his lived experiences and advocate for what he and his staff needed to make even more significant advances with their student body, families, and the surrounding community.

The committee was comprised of district curriculum and instruction, pupil services, specialized services, strategic planning, assessment, and finance directors. One of the state requirements for this team was that principals be included. Mr. Jones was joined by another high school principal colleague and four elementary principals. His other colleagues were also selected based on improved academic success, building culture, and climate improvement. The first task was to develop goals based on the student achievement data. The strategic planning director worked with the assessment data director to present the data they recommended considering in the goal-setting process.

Mr. Jones and his colleagues were highly familiar with their schools' data because they had a close network that shared strategies for improvement. The principals monitored their data using the state Department of Instruction dashboard, which provided test scores directly from the testing company. When the district assessment director presented the data, the principals were stunned because it was incorrect for each school. The information did not match the data from the state dashboard. The principals wondered if the data was incorrect for their schools and how accurate it was for the rest of the district, which only increased their concerns about the inaccuracies. However, the strategic planning and assessment directors insisted that the data was correct. Meanwhile, the strategic planning director had already prepared the five goals he wanted to include in the INOI state plan. Mr. Jones quickly realized that the principals had been invited only as a matter of state compliance and not necessarily to contribute their expertise.

One of the significant advancements Mr. Jones and his staff made was related to Black male student achievement. To make these improvements, Mr. Jones had his staff disaggregate achievement data by gender and race so they could understand how their current instruction impacted each specific population. They also began professional development to address implicit biases and to shift from deficit-based to asset-based approaches. Finally, they spent a great deal of time embedding culturally responsive teaching strategies within their instruction to meet the needs of their Black male students.

When Mr. Jones shared his school's journey in supporting improved student achievement for Black males, the directors seemed uncomfortable (ICK-quity). Mr. Jones said that as they analyzed the school's data, they realized Black males needed more equitable resources and strategies to improve their performance. As the committee analyzed the district data, Mr. Jones noticed a similar trend for the entire district. He was excited to share his feedback to support a plan to help improve performance for Black boys across the district. However, the directors did not want to highlight the gap between Black male students and other racial and gender groups for fear of appearing biased toward one group by giving more attention and resources to support improvement. So, they only agreed to disaggregate the achievement data by gender and by white students versus *all* boys of color, not Black boys specifically. Stunned at this decision, Mr. Jones helped them to see that it would be disingenuous to represent the data in this way because Asian male students vastly outperformed white males. Latino/x boys were mostly on par with white male students, while Black boys were significantly below all-male student achievement. Yet, they disregarded his observations and analysis and developed the goals based on the general findings. The following are examples of misguided analyses that were carried out:

Avoidance Analysis:

> The directors wanted to circumvent calling out Black males as the lowest performing students because they feared the political backlash of parents. They tried to protect the district from the negative press that would say they had not been appropriately educating Black males. They also feared that their more affluent, white parents would think that resources would be shifted from their children to Black boys.

Misinformation Analysis:

> The school board and district administration had recently become leery of discussing issues of race in professional development. This shift came due to proposed legislation to ban DEI content in workplace training. The administration feared making teachers in the district "uncomfortable" if they discussed mitigating implicit bias and deficit thinking regarding Black males. Several school board directors also thought that culturally responsive teaching was Critical Race Theory, and they were *not* having any of it in their district. They gave incorrect information about the data that would be used to make the critical decisions about the goals they needed to secure the additional resources from the state.

Dialing Back Equity Progress Analysis:

> Finally, now that the district directors understood what Mr. Jones was doing in his school, they shared their concerns with the superintendent about the potential backlash that could arise. As a result, Mr. Jones was asked to stop his professional development on implicit bias.

HOW CAN MR. JONES PUSH THROUGH THIS WHITE STATE?

Mr. Jones has been a true warrior for equity in the context of his school. However, he faces many barriers, ramping up his efforts to impact more students district-wide. Mr. Jones has several factors that work in his favor to push through the obstacles presented in this scenario. He has already had experience successfully shifting the mindset of teachers about students with low achievement. The kind of professional development he has done in his school was proven to impact student performance positively.

Since Mr. Jones must undergo some discussions about his professional development, he can be prepared with the data to demonstrate how he and his curriculum leaders facilitate the content and provide suggestions on how the district could do so.

Another key factor that Mr. Jones has on his side is that he is part of a network of other principals focused on student success. So, he does not have to be a lone wolf advocating for the changes needed. At this point, he and the other principals need to consider what advocates they have at the central service level who may have more influence.

Given the resistance that Mr. Jones is facing, he should prioritize what is most important. Correcting the data being analyzed to create the goals is perhaps the most important. Second, creating goals based on accurate data would be important. This impacts how and where the state resources will be used and where they will be allocated.

In education and other industries, several tough decisions need to be made in a timely manner to meet deadlines. While gaining insight from those close to the work is ideal and always recommended, those in leadership often aim to be decisive to make decisions by deadlines. Decision-making usually becomes more complicated as more voices are added. In this scenario, the hard truth is that the agenda was already set when the team's work began. Unbeknownst to the committee, their unspoken expectation was to rubber-stamp the goals.

Mr. Jones must consider what actions he is willing to take to push against the constraints in this situation. Ruffling the feathers of the directors leading this committee could have adverse consequences for Mr. Jones and his career. He could be vocal about these issues or think about ways to influence those who could change the situation. Mr. Jones could also utilize the principal network to impact the school goals instead of aiming for the visible district-wide goal. He could work with the other principals to disaggregate their schools' data to set equitable school goals.

Finally, Mr. Jones may have to consider the T (timing) in his ICE-T. There may be some things that Mr. Jones decides to document and be prepared to share at a different time. In this situation, those in charge are fixed on their agenda. While unfortunate, the agenda may play out, and decisions may be made that do not contribute to more equitable outcomes for the students who need the most support and resources. Mr. Jones must ask himself if ensuring the work is done within his sphere of influence is enough. He was recruited for this committee because of how he and his team successfully improved student achievement for all, even those with more challenging data, at his school. He may have to accept that his input was muted at the district level but continue working to improve the education of the students in his school. However, in due time, the opportunity could arise where those with decision-making power will want to take heed of Mr. Jones's expertise.

Questions to Consider

1. In your work setting, what are known inequities that have clear solutions people consistently avoid addressing? What solutions have been offered to addressing these inequities? Why has the inequity not been addressed?
2. In what ways have misinformation and failure to correct it impacted issues of inequity within your work setting? Who has been most impacted by the misinformation?
3. What are efforts or initiatives within your work setting that have improved inequities for marginalized people or groups? Describe specific efforts that have intentionally dialed back the progress made.
4. In your context, identify identifiers that are associated with the White Phase. What are the most pressing identifiers. Given your ICE-T, in what ways can you recalibrate those in the setting to consider taking more equitable actions?
5. What calculated risks are you willing to take to redirect others to take more equitable actions? What are you not willing to do to address the issues of inequity within your setting? Why or why not?

CHAPTER 4

The Light Gray Phase

Not everything that is faced can be changed, but nothing can be changed until it is faced.

—James Baldwin

In chapter 3, we described the White Phase of the Equity Empowerment Continuum. Avoidance, providing misinformation, and dialing back progress stop equitable outcomes. It may be clear that those seeking to be more equitable would not engage in these actions or behaviors. The next part of the EEC, the Light Gray Phase, holds up a mirror to the work individuals and organizations are doing in the name of equity. The Light Gray Phase identifiers' named efforts often fail to create sustainable, long-lasting, equitable changes. The light gray identifiers include being performative allies, over-analysis, and "kicking the can down the road."

When considering the Light Gray Phase, it is unclear whether individuals mean to make a true change or if it is to make an appearance of change. Light gray actions generally imply performative equity work. A few years ago, when I began my position as an equity leader, I was on Facebook and came across a post by Dr. Paul Gorski. He has written several books and articles about equity in schools, has facilitated equity-related professional development, and often delivers workshops and keynote speeches on equity. In his post, he referred to what many school districts were doing for equity work as "Equity Light." This concept resonated with me and made me think of when I was a kid in the 1980s. Many beverage companies had products filled with a lot of sugar, but as people became more conscious of calorie intake and weight loss, the companies started to produce sodas/pops with substitute sweeteners, which we all know as "light" drinks now. The companies tried to market it as having the same good taste but fewer calories. Thinking of this, I posted that many districts were doing "diet equity." Just like soda/pop companies go to great lengths to convince consumers that their diet drinks have the same good taste with less caloric impact, individuals and organizations that operate in the Light Gray Phase try to do equity work without the extra ingredients that make it impactful and meaningful. They want the public to believe they are doing real equity work, yet their efforts are much less than needed to match their espoused impact on marginalized people and communities. Sometimes, this dissonance is intentional. But, other times, this behavior is often unconsciously carried out.

PERFORMATIVE ALLYSHIP

Allyship can be an essential vehicle for equitable change. An ally is a colleague or organization that uses their privileged identity or power to support the cause of a marginalized person or group. This is commendable. However, many who want the commendations of allyship do not want the work that goes along with it. Instead, they abandon the work, and this support turns into a *performative* allyship. As Morris (2020) of *Forbes Magazine* describes it:

> Performative allyship . . . is where those with privilege, profess solidarity with a cause. This assumed solidarity is usually vocalized, disingenuous, and potentially harmful to marginalized groups. Often, the performative ally professes allegiance in order to distance themselves from potential scrutiny. In many cases, organizational leaders use performance-driven activity in a way that they believe will protect the company brand from being highlighted in a negative way. It is often referred to by Black employees and their supporters as 'talking the talk, without walking the walk."

One example of performative allyship from an individual perspective is when people post things on social media about injustice, but, in real life, choose not to speak about injustice to family or friends. In their work setting, they do not address injustice even if they have the privilege to influence or make a change. As it relates to organizations, performative allyship is when the organization attempts to *appear* socially conscious and oriented toward social justice but does not fully understand the inequitable or oppressive actions that it perpetuates. However, they feel it necessary to join the bandwagon of public statements to appear socially conscious.

"RONA AND RACISM": JUMPING ON THE MISSION STATEMENT BANDWAGON

According to the official Black Lives Matter (BLM, n.d.) website, the BLM movement began with the acquittal of George Zimmerman, who killed Trayvon Martin, a seventeen-year-old teenager walking home from the store at night. In May 2020, during the initial pandemic shutdown, a perfect storm was born that one of my Facebook friends called "Rona and racism." The combination of people cooped up in their homes due to the coronavirus pandemic and the viral cell phone video of the in-your-face murder of George Floyd in broad daylight created a nexus where individuals, organizations, and companies could no longer ignore the blatant abuse of people of color by the police.

After millions of people worldwide took to the streets to protest the murder of George Floyd, many who would never have found themselves in the middle of a protest were in the middle of rallies. Some of these new zealots had never publicly discussed issues of racism before. Many were even accustomed to avoiding sensitive conversations about politics with their families in fear of insulting relatives who were known racists, sexists, or bigots of some kind. Yet, with newfound revelations about systemic racism and institutional power confronting them, new "woke folks" began to question police, government, and workplace practices that allowed these awful deeds to continue without consequence. This new awakening put pressure on companies to take a position or a stand against injustice in allegiance with the BLM movement and, in a hurried rush, many companies put together statements about their support. However, most companies or organizations had never mentioned the movement before. Some had policies and practices that were antithetical to

BLM. Such public statements can be mistaken for actual equity work meant to bring about substantial and sustainable change. Yet without internal practices, policies, and procedures demonstrating actual commitment, the actions are performative and light gray with minimal impact. This is true for individuals and organizations alike.

Performative allyship is often misconstrued as progress. Many companies or organizational statements are issued to make people feel that change is happening. For example, after the murder of George Floyd, the phrase Black Lives Matter became a part of our global vocabulary. Whereas, a few years before George Floyd's murder, this term was seen as fringe in most spaces. Eight years earlier, in 2012, the school board of directors in the district where I was hired to lead equity work held a progressive position related to the BLM movement. After the murder of Trayvon Martin, the board unanimously passed a resolution supporting BLM. While acknowledging the broad injustice to Black people in society, the resolution sought to increase awareness about the low achievement and high discipline rates for Black students. Very few people knew that the district had passed this resolution and funded this new initiative. To inform my independent work, I included the resolution in some of the professional learning I facilitated. Although the statement could be seen as performative, I used it as a directive from the board of directors. In some respects, the initiative to increase awareness about achievement and discipline rates gave the message more weight.

"NO JUSTICE! NO JAVA!" STARBUCKS STRUGGLES TO ALIGN WITH ITS MISSION

While the company's mission statement has always embraced inclusivity, Starbucks has struggled to realize its mission. Starbucks has long taken heat about its participation in gentrifying communities of color (Somaiya, 2015). Rethink Retail (2020) describes how communities have typically viewed an incoming Starbucks as an indicator that property values will increase and become unaffordable to longtime residents. Over time, they have become a symbol of displacement in these communities.

While settling several of its internal racial discrimination challenges, a few public bouts with racism gained significant attention. In Milwaukee, Wisconsin, in 2014, a Starbucks employee called the police on a man sleeping on a bench near the Red Arrow Park store (Luthern, 2015). The call ended in the police officer shooting and killing Dontray Hamilton, a Black man with documented mental health challenges. After protests and national news attention earned the company significant negative press, efforts to mitigate their poor image ensued. In 2015, Starbucks launched its "Race Together" initiative, where the management asked the baristas to either put "Race Together" stickers or write race conversation starter phrases on customers' cups (The Outline, n.d.). Some saw the campaign as shameless publicity, while others recognized the positive intention but critiqued the missteps in execution. Asking your staff to initiate conversations about race that could quickly turn awkward, uncomfortable, or even dangerous, is an ill-conceived approach at best. The fierce outrage expressed by the public caused an abrupt end to the campaign.

While Starbucks continued its strategy to improve its racial equity reputation, other major anti-Black snafus occurred in Starbucks stores. In April 2018, two Black men were arrested in Philadelphia after an employee called the police on them because they asked to use the bathroom and remained in the store without purchasing an item (Neuman, 2018). Other white guests were observed doing the same thing but did not have the police called on them. A few days later, another Black man had the police called on him because he questioned why a white customer was allowed to access the locked bathroom before his purchase and he was not. Fortunately, he was not arrested. However, these incidents sparked more national outrage against the billion-dollar company.

Performative actions are often put into place in the hope that public missteps are forgotten, and further reputation damage is mitigated. Organizations and leaders must understand the issues affecting them and develop a strategic plan based on continuous improvement to avoid performative actions. This means establishing a plan, setting goals, evaluating progress, and taking corrective action based on results data. To Starbucks' credit, they course-corrected their Race Together plan by halting it once they realized that the public did not receive it well and the campaign caused unintended harm.

Starbucks also refined some of its earlier performative actions by supplementing its statements with community investments and resources. These darker gray actions, which we will explore in detail in the next chapter, offered substantial economic relief for the urban spaces Starbucks had entered as gentrifiers. The company has since hired a Diversity CEO to further drive these efforts. The *Philidelphia Business Journal* reported that, by 2025, the Starbucks Community Resilience Fund will commit $100 million to support small business and community development initiatives in neighborhoods that have had long-standing challenges securing financial resources (Fuhrmeister, 2021).

They also joined the Board Diversity Action Alliance (n.d.), a coalition of major corporations that includes PNC Bank, Uber, PepsiCo, and UPS. The Alliance aims to drive accountability measures within member companies to increase the diversity on their corporate boards of directors and to report progress on equity benchmarks annually. These actions provide more substance. Instead of just talking about racism or hoping to eliminate it with coffee cup mottos, their commitment to resources, staffing, and investments in communities of color deepens their engagement with the issues that make inequity possible in the first place.

Even still, some may say this is not enough, and more is needed to prove that this company is committed to social justice. Many employees have long reported poor working conditions and a need to unionize. These efforts have been met with resistance until February 2024. Greenhouse (2024) of *The Guardian* reports that efforts to unionize were finally agreed to by Starbucks management in 2024. Other critics also charge that Starbucks has a superficial commitment to "ethically sourced products" (Angel, 2021). The Coffee Barometer, a global organization, asserts that coffee companies like Starbucks are not doing enough to ensure environmental health in production and protect human rights. While Starbucks has tried to align its actions with an inclusive mission, it remains under scrutiny as to whether the efforts are enough or just performative allyship.

REFLECTION

Reflect on a time when you noticed performative allyship within your organization or community. How did you address it, or what could you do differently in future situations to push for authentic action?

OVERANALYSIS OVERLOAD: HOW EQUITY WORK STALLED

Another light gray identifier is when individuals or organizations participate in superficial over-analysis of equity problems. Many organizations subscribe to continuous improvement models to strategically address challenges that require change. Typically, these models include four steps. First, the problem must be identified. Second, a plan of action must be developed. Third, the plan must be executed. And finally, an analysis of the completed plan must be conducted to determine its impact and whether the organization's goals were met. If not, employees are often expected to take on additional work or to propose and implement a new course of action, thus making the process continuous.

Equity work can easily get caught between the first and second steps. Organizations often identify that there is some kind of problem, especially in our current climate, with the proliferation of DEI positions in almost every industry. In some senses, it's easy to see the necessity of introspection and investigating policies and practices that lead to inequitable outcomes. Before the decision to allocate resources to DEI is even made, organizations often already understand which marginalized communities have not been adequately employed or positioned in leadership positions, and many are also aware that they have yet to serve their diverse clientele as well as they should, whether they are citizens, business clients, medical patients, or students. It's likely the data already exists. However, the work of DEI leaders is often misappropriated. For instance, they are frequently asked to lead committees that "study" the problem. Such studies typically show that the inequities within the organization are precisely what people expect them to be. They may need additional data, but sometimes they are aware, and these additional "studies" are a stall tactic so that the leadership can find a way to frame the inequities to the staff and/or the public.

As teams convene over weeks, possibly years, they determine that more research is needed. With more research comes more consultants who tell the organization more about what they already know: They are fostering an inequitable environment in the workplace. As this additional analysis is taking place, there could very well be turnover in leadership, which requires briefing new staff on the inequities and what has been done to address them to that point. By this time, years may have passed, and nothing has been done to address the inequity beyond the attempt to understand it, which is not a guarantee. Meanwhile, leaders in the organization can point to all the efforts that are taking place to address the inequities. They can say things like, "We have an equity committee that's looking at those issues at this very moment." To be clear, I am not saying that you can do equity work without research. But I am saying that formulating long-term strategic plans to address long-standing problems is sometimes a way to avoid addressing the inequities at all. The plans become ends in themselves and the resolutions get lost in the details.

Year to year, many school districts across the country continue to examine horrific data about historically marginalized students. I have sat in countless meetings where our task was to examine the data related to disproportionality in student achievement, engagement, discipline, and other factors contributing to low performance in education. One of my colleagues used to call it "data-gazing." In these meetings, it is almost as if we celebrate the data. These data show exactly what is already known. This ongoing analysis is stuck in stage one of the continuous model. This is where the problem is studied. But if studying the problem is where this process always lives, we don't ever get to address the issue.

REFLECTION

In your organization, how long does data-gathering typically take when addressing a challenge? How is that data utilized in decision-making to advance equity?

KICKING THE CAN DOWN THE ROAD

"Kicking the Can" (Merriam-Webster, 2023) became a popular game played by children during the Great Depression when there was little money to purchase store-bought games. The premise is like hide-and-seek where everyone hides, and one person seeks them out. Whoever is found becomes the next seeker. In "Kick the Can," if someone hiding can kick a tin can without being caught by the seeker, then everyone hiding is set free. This concept developed into "kicking the can down the road," a commonly used idiom today that describes when people fail to address something by avoiding or delaying their response. In the case of equity work, this means knowing an issue or challenge exists but deciding that someone else down the "road" will address it.

Often, when people take on positions as equity leaders, they do not truly understand the real equity challenges the organization is facing. When you interview for a job, no one tells you about the numerous challenges that you will face dismantling all the long-standing and systematic marginalization that has and continues to occur. Hiring teams frequently have faith that the "can" will stop with you, the new leader. Their hope is that you will provide the magic bullet that answers every persistent organizational inequity.

When I stepped into the equity position from the professoriate, I thought I had a magic bullet. As an assistant professor, I studied, researched, and taught about inequities in urban school districts. But I was only truly able to understand the challenges districts faced once I began to examine their data from the inside and talk with leaders, coworkers, teachers, families, and students who were most impacted by the district's inequities. It is one thing to read about the racial disparities in academic achievement, but then another to go into an advanced placement classroom and see that despite being a predominantly Black school, not a single Black student was enrolled.

Similarly, one of my social justice research areas was related to providing more gender-inclusive spaces in schools. I have studied and even published a few papers on the topic. I understood that resistance to implementing best practices for LGBTQ students was typically prevalent among staff. I did not truly understand this resistance, however, until I facilitated training about how to make schools more inclusive and some people walked out saying, "This [LGBTQ training] is not a part of my job!" I came to understand that the "can" for gender-inclusive social justice had been kicked down the road for many years. While in the role, I was able to pull together work that previous advocates had done and revise the nondiscrimination policy to be more gender inclusive. A major part of this work was to make sure that the entire district understood what best practices were in serving students and staff.

Regardless of what industry or position you find yourself in, you must identify the "cans" and put a stop to "kicking them down the road." Even if you believe you understand equity challenges from previous research and studies, you must gain an authentic sense of the challenges once you are in the organization. There is an old adage that says, "It may not be your fault, but it is your responsibility." This means that while you may not have been a part of the inequities that exist, you must address them if you want to be considered an equity leader. You must do things that will directly or indirectly impact the system where you work.

But how do organizations get to this point in the first place? What can be done to prevent the can from tumbling down the road in the first place? "Kicking the can down the road" happens when organizations lack a stable, committed plan. A consistent leader with a plan and resources are needed to make equitable changes within the organization.

PUTTING THE WRONG PERSON IN THE RIGHT SEAT

Selecting the wrong leaders to lead equity efforts will always delay and frustrate meaningful change. With the explosion of the need for people to fill equity roles, many candidates have applied to roles who are inexperienced or otherwise unable to lead systemic, organization-wide equity efforts. Gupta (2021) has noted a pattern of hiring BIPOC individuals for these roles simply because they can often relate to the marginalization the hiring organization seeks to dismantle. Within the medical profession, many faculty members who take on equity positions tend to be young or new to their career and lacking the formal education and training necessary for the role (Vela et al., 2021). But this isn't limited to the medical world. Many organizations across professions are hiring people with valuable and legitimate lived experience, but little capacity to support professional development or to develop a strategic plan for implementing sustainable change.

NO MONEY WHERE YOUR MOUTH IS

Almost as bad as putting the wrong person in the right seat is under-resourcing equity work. In organizations with longstanding inequities, hiring someone alone will not turn the tide. While many organizations offer equity positions, sometimes they are solo positions without proper staff and resources. In cases like these, the officers are often asked to be a jack of all trades **and** a master of all of them too. Initially, when I was hired as the equity leader, I was the sole person relegated to that work in a school district of seventy thousand students and five thousand employees. One intern was assigned to work with me. Fortunately, the intern had a broad capacity and was able to significantly help and co-lead a lot of the work. My job was to provide support to departments across the organization. As a school educator and administrator, I had formal training in many things related to the general curriculum and school-level leadership. There were areas where I had little to no experience, yet I had to be the equity authority to validate decisions and planning. I provided a new level of equity awareness within the organization. But without additional formal resources, it became clear that my impact would be limited. After I left this position and joined another department, the district realized it needed additional resources and support to keep the organization focused on changing its equity trajectory. The district hired a new equity person but made my successor a director and aligned staff to support their work. The ideal scenario is always to have equity leaders supported by an adequate number of staff who have the knowledge and capacity to realize the group's equity visions and put its plans into place.

In summary, if you find that you or your organization are making statements about social justice but not taking *substantive* actions to make equity a reality in the organization, the efforts are light gray. If you are spending time analyzing and reanalyzing inequity with committees and unqualified or under-resourced leadership, your actions are light gray. If you or your organization understands the barriers that exist in righting historical and persistent wrongs but continue to "kick the can down the road" for someone in the future to address, the efforts are light gray.

If your actions are light gray identifiers, moving toward the Dark Gray Phase must be your goal. You can't just talk about equity; you must be about equity, which means you must do something. Individuals and organizations often critique the actions of others. The key to taking more substantial actions toward equity and justice is to step outside of the status quo. These actions will likely feel and be uncomfortable. But if you or your organization want to make meaningful changes, you must embrace that discomfort and remember that many came before us who cared enough about the future to be uncomfortable and make sacrifices. It is up to you to take risks and use your sphere of control and influence to bend the arc closer to justice.

Chapters 3 and 4 describe how the white and light gray phases impede movement toward more equitable outcomes. As an equity leader, you do not want your actions to fall into these categories, but many factors can contribute to you or your organization operating in the light gray. In pushing through this phase of equity, you must determine how to use both your ICE-T and spheres of influence and control. You must also be willing to take risks and commit to building capacity for such risk-taking. The following vignette exemplifies how a well-intended leader may unintentionally perpetuate light-gray actions, followed by considering how one could strategically push through this shade of gray to more impactful actions.

END-OF-CHAPTER CONSIDERATIONS: LIGHTLY LEADING THE "EQUITY" COMMITTEE

An individual's ICE-T often informs why their well-intentioned actions are functionally light gray. Kristen was recently asked to lead a DEI committee in her department. Her ICE-T consists of being a white woman (identity) who has been looked over within her department for promotions. Kristen recently discovered that she is being paid 10 percent less than her white male counterpart (context). In her attempt to advocate for herself, she realized that speaking up quickly gets her shut down and further marginalized within the department (experience). Since she had taken an advocacy stance and made it clear that she wanted to take on more leadership, her supervisor begrudgingly asked her to lead the equity committee for the department even though the organization is three years out from the creation of their 2020 DEI statements for fostering more equitable environments (timing).

Given this ICE-T, Kristen must determine to what extent she will risk her current reputation, which is a bit cantankerous with the leadership team. While she completely understands the issues related to gender equity, she does not understand the challenges and concerns of others on the committee. Kristen does not quite see the issues and disparities related to her Black and Brown colleagues, who experience an even larger gap in pay with even less representation at the senior leadership level. She is also an extremely devout Christian who has strong beliefs about marriage being between a man and a woman only. She does not understand preferred pronouns and what any of the letters beyond LGB mean in the acronym LGBTQIA+ (identity).

The leadership charge for the committee is to identify areas of inequities and provide guidance to the leadership team on how to address them. Kristen begins her work by sending out an open call to the whole department requesting volunteers to serve on the much-needed equity committee. However, she also wants to ensure that she attracts members to the committee who understand the existing gender inequities. Even though a diverse group of people respond to the call, Kristen personally reaches out to the other white women interested in understanding how they could be promoted and receive equitable pay.

As the committee's work gets underway, the team has difficulty coming together on its focus and goals. A few Muslim members want to discuss issues related to food choices in the cafeteria and unspoken "rules" about dress codes and restrictions to wearing hijabs. A transgender woman who has not shared their gender identity within the company submits a request to the committee to create more gender neutrality within the organization. Additionally, several Black and Brown committee members ask to address the recurrent and long-standing issues they have faced for several years, including discriminatory hiring, promotion practices, and low retention rates. Clearly, the "can" had been "kicked down the road" for a long time.

Over several months, the committee meets and accomplishes little because each meeting is contentious, with varying angles the committee members want to focus on pulling the group in different directions. Based on Kristen's unfavorable experiences speaking up about gender inequities in the past, she sought to take a more timid approach to advocating for some of the committee's concerns, especially those **she** did not understand. Though Kristen was a naturally strong facilitator, her passion for addressing gender issues overtakes her ability to represent everyone in the group and organization. Whenever issues other than gender are presented, a subcommittee is appointed to study past trends related to that topic even though intel already exists (over analysis).

Many of the committee members fail to understand their Muslim colleagues' concerns. However, they attempt to offer comfort and support by mentioning some of the challenges they face with what the organization calls "professional dress" in the workplace. Some of the white women talk about being reprimanded for wearing certain "revealing" outfits. A few Black committee members discussed the dilemmas they face on whether to wear their natural hair to work or not. However, no one wants to include these concerns within the committee platform. The committee understands the importance of recalibrating professionalism standards to be more inclusive.

However, they believe that it will make the leaders too uncomfortable. With that, the committee empathizes with the Muslim colleagues but fails to include the concern within the agenda (performative allyship).

Those outside of the department who were not on the equity committee begin to think that nothing will result from the committee because they do not see any changes being made. While the equity committee was well-intentioned, it makes little to no progress.

HOW CAN KRISTEN AND HER TEAM PUSH THROUGH THIS SHADE OF LIGHT GRAY?

Kristen has the potential to be an excellent equity leader. While experiencing inequity can be detrimental and traumatizing, it can also remind us of the inequities and inequalities that persist in our work environments and society at large. These experiences become opportunities to make positive changes for ourselves and others. While she knows firsthand what it feels like to be oppressed because of gender, she must consider the experiences of others on the equity committee. To PUSH through the shades of gray, she must be willing to hear about the multiple identities, experiences, and contexts of those on her committee so she can understand the depth and breadth of the inequities that exist. Pushing through for Kristen means that she must embrace Dr. King's mantra, "Injustice anywhere is a threat to justice everywhere...Whatever affects one directly affects all indirectly." While gender equity is at the top of her mind, many of the other challenges experienced in her department have contributed to the overall oppressive environment. If the team can see how the injustices they have experienced are linked and mutually reinforcing, they can manifest collective progress.

Kristen and her team can push through this light-gray position is by "sipping from others' ICE-T." Instead of viewing the multiple perspectives as a barrier, Kristen and the team should view their diversity as a lever. Progress can be made by spreading out the leadership responsibilities and building upon the strengths of others' ICE-T. Effective efforts in equity only occur when it becomes the work of multiple stakeholders. Understanding that Kristen may have a somewhat challenging relationship with leadership, she should determine who on the committee can be a true ally with a more positive influence when interacting with the leadership team. Moreover, depending on what issues this team chooses to champion, they should strategically determine who should lead which aspects of each cause. While Kristen may be most passionate about gender equity, a true ally on the team who may not have had the same context and experience can lend a different perspective, demonstrating a broader need to make critical changes to the current structures.

Furthermore, this team would do well by adopting and adhering to norms or agreements that would enable Kristen, as well as all team members, to push themselves to hear and understand all the equity concerns and perspectives. While the issues that need to be addressed are about more than just race, Singleton's (2022) Courageous Conversations about Race (CCAR) protocol would be a useful tool to provide an opportunity for Kristen and all committee members to hear and understand multiple perspectives. The four agreements from that protocol are as follows: staying engaged, speaking your truth, experiencing discomfort, and accepting and expecting non-closure. Such protocols can anchor discussions to keep the team together and on track. These agreements, coupled with strong facilitation skills, can support the team in developing immediate, intermediary, and long-term goals. The CCAR tool also has a compass that enables different people to enter conversations from various perspectives, which does not make other perspectives better or worse. The compass gives individuals an opportunity to reflect on their own entry points and foster mutual respect with others to move the team forward.

Finally, oftentimes equity committee work is volunteer work, which means time is limited, individuals often lack capacity to act, and accomplishments come slowly. Those passionate about addressing these issues are likely to have other job responsibilities. Kristen may have to advocate for additional compensation or work release for those working on this committee. If neither option is possible, it will become critical for Kristen and her team to communicate effectively about the work being done, given the resources and capacity they have. Having a committee work on equity can be light gray without the proper resources and communication with the larger department or organization.

In sum, good intentions are not always the best intentions. In this vignette, Kristen had a specific area where she desired to see change within her work setting. However, she was unable to see the struggles of her colleagues within this space. Pushing through to see and embrace marginalization in different contexts and times is central to the work that Kristen and her team must do both individually and as a collective committee.

If this chapter has described you or your work, your goal should be to consider ways to shift your mindset and actions further along the EEC, where authentic change is strengthened and reinforced by sustainability. We will discuss such mindsets and actions in the following chapters.

Questions to Consider

1. What equity issue (at work or in general) are you most passionate about and know the most about? What are some equity areas that you feel less knowledgeable about? How can you learn more about these issues?
2. To date, what discovery work to understand inequities has already occurred in your organization? How can that work inform the development of a plan to address those inequities? Are there already plans to address inequities that can be expanded and/or executed?
3. What is my ICE-T? How does my ICE-T benefit me in advancing equitable actions? How does my ICE-T stifle efforts toward creating more equitable outcomes?
4. Who else in your network is passionate about equity and can support your efforts as an ally?
5. What grounding norms and agreements do you have for challenging yourself and others to discuss difficult conversations about inequities within your workplace or in general?
6. Do you have the right people in the right positions and the money (or resources) you need to adequately address inequities? If not, what is the plan to address those needs? Who in your network can support this plan? What barriers might you face?

CHAPTER 5

The Dark Gray Phase

In 2019, I was honored to receive the "To Do What Is Just" Award from the Milwaukee Innercity Congregations Allied for Hope (MICAH). This community faith-based organization works to build bridges with multiple congregations by collaborating on social issues that impact all communities. I was honored and humbled by the recognition because many previous winners had significant roles in the city's fight for justice. When I was first notified, I reflected on why an award needed to be created to recognize "just" work. In my mind, everybody should always try to do what is just, and I would like to think that, on my leadership journey, I had always done what was "just." Whether that was leading the equity initiative in my district, serving students in a K-12 classroom, being a middle school administrator, or advising leadership candidates as an assistant professor, I always wanted to make the right call or do what was "just." The truth of the matter is I fell short at times. I was honored for my "just" work. However, I also knew that sometimes, I did not stand up for what was right either because it was too hard at the time or I did not know how. Dr. King said, "The time is always right to do the right thing." However, as noted in the previous chapters, we often fail to "do the right thing."

This chapter explores the Dark Gray Phase, which involves working within a system to understand its nuances and tensions to create equitable changes. Even though the Dark Gray Phase will be described here, it is important first to introduce what distinguishes this phase from the Black Phase, which will be explained

FIGURE 5.1 • The Equity Empowerment Continuum (Dark Gray/Black Interaction)

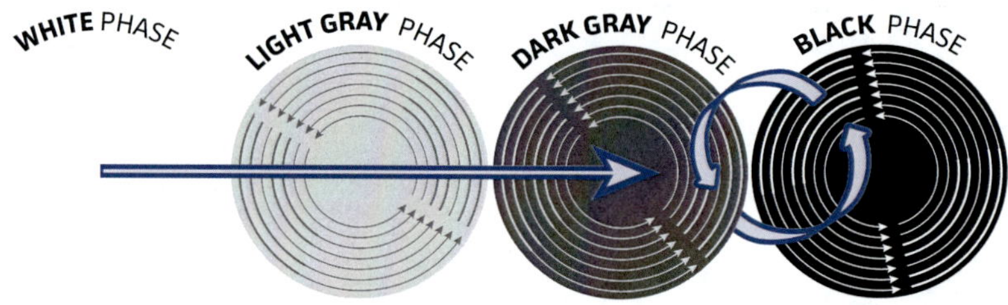

Graphic by Molly Quirk

in detail in the next chapter. One of the Black Phase identifiers is having comprehensive codifications in place to protect the rights of all people and groups. These are large-scale actions and/or decisions that impact the whole society. In contrast, written accountability addresses equality and equity within a particular context like a school district, governmental agency, or corporation. In the Black Phase, comprehensive codifications are large-scale decisions and/or actions that lead to justice for marginalized people and/or groups.

The Black Phase informs how people advocate and achieve equity within their personal, work, local, or community context. In the Dark Gray Phase, those advocating for equity draw from the decisions and actions produced in the Black Phase. The constant interplay between these two phases will be discussed in greater detail in chapter 6. The Black Phase is aspirational, and the Dark Gray Phase is actionable. In the end, your work should be both aspirational and actionable.

I could be a perpetual optimist, but I believe that deep at most people's core, they seek to do the most just thing in every situation. The hope to do what is right or just also extends to our work setting. However, we often struggle to do equity work, which presents multiple challenges and barriers to change. The Black Phase is foundational to bolstering equity work. However, the Dark Gray Phase is the reality of executing justice within the context of your work.

The Dark Gray Phase identifiers include maximizing your spheres of influence and control, using ICE-T to create Win-Wins, and creating accountability systems to monitor and ensure implementation and sustainability.

MAXIMIZE YOUR SPHERES OF INFLUENCE AND CONTROL

To reiterate, the C in "ICE-T" stands for the context. Understanding how changes are accomplished in the context is essential to understanding the Dark Gray Phase. This book has outlined the many challenges of implementing equity. As noted in the White Phase, because of people's personal ICK-quity, they avoid issues to escape political backlash and misinformation and concerted efforts to dial back progress. To overcome ICK-quity, you must be strategic. There are spheres of influence you must consider as you try to impact any change. That's a fundamental concept in personal development, leadership, and decision-making.

Aguilar (2014), a well-known education coach guru, discusses "the spheres of control" to help people understand where they should put their energy into solving perceived challenges (See figure 5.2). The sphere of influence refers to the areas of life or work over which they can exert significant control or influence. It encompasses things that directly affect them or that they have the power to affect. For example, a building principal might have a sphere of influence over her staff, teaching and learning, student programming, and family engagement. The school leaders can also influence the staff to adopt and implement certain policies or strategies that impact the immediate school community.

FIGURE 5.2 • Spheres of Influence and Control

Graphic by Molly Quirk

You must act on things within your sphere of control. You make the call. It includes actions, decisions, behaviors, and resources within your power to manage or manipulate. For example, a department chair has discretion in the department budget and curriculum. They can allocate funding to support additional services for students who need more support. From a personal standpoint, this might include your attitudes, actions, and responses to situations. Expressing an equitable mindset and openness to shifting away from old practices signals to the staff an equity expectation in how your department does business.

While you may not want to admit it, some things are outside your control. There are aspects of life or circumstances an individual or organization cannot directly influence or control. These could be external factors such as natural disasters, other people's actions, global economic trends, or unexpected events. While these factors may still impact someone's life or environment, they are beyond their immediate ability to change or manipulate.

As you personally decide how you or your team will enact equitable actions, understanding these distinctions can help you focus your efforts and energy on the areas that can make the most difference. At the same time, you can also accept and adapt to those aspects of life that are beyond your control.

UNLIKELY CANDIDATE BECOMES FIRST BLACK PRESIDENT

Whether you are a Democrat, a Republican, or an Independent, the story of Barack Obama becoming the first Black president in the US is a perfect example of how you can effectively use spheres of influence and control. After forty-three white male presidents, in 2008, Barack Obama was elected the first Black president. His path to the presidency in 2008 was characterized by political skill, grassroots mobilization, strategic messaging, and coalition building. His unprecedented navigation of his spheres of control and influence enabled him to overcome the odds to clinch the Democratic nomination and be elected as the first Black US president.

THINGS WITHIN HIS SPHERE OF INFLUENCE AND CONTROL

Political candidates address platforms and planks during their campaigns. As candidates run for president, they must establish a campaign based on their political party's platform that details how they will lead. Teaching Democracy (2024) defines a party platform as "a set of principles, goals, and strategies designed to address pressing political issues" (*Political Parties Platforms - Election Central - Political Parties, Platforms, and Planks,* 2024). Then, planks provide details that address specific issues. What is within the candidate's sphere of control and influence is how they will address the platform and particular issues. For example, accessible healthcare is an important plank of the Democratic party platform. Gottlieb (2024) recounts how President Obama elevated healthcare in this campaign. Candidate Senator Hillary Clinton, his formidable opponent, laid the groundwork for healthcare but missed the mark when her bill dubbed "Hillarycare" was not brought to a vote in Congress in 1994. After Obama was elected, Congress would ultimately pass the Affordable Care Act, which reduced the number of uninsured Americans and lowered healthcare costs. Obama learned from the Clintons' healthcare reform efforts, adopting a more strategic approach that led to the successful passage of the Affordable Care Act. Their earlier work helped shape public support, paving the way for his success. Building upon existing work to move closer to your desired results is crucial.

Additionally, Barack Obama's improbable journey from a presidential underdog to securing the Democratic nomination and eventually the US presidency in 2008 was marked by the strategic utilization of various spheres of influence and control. Senator Barack Obama had significant political acumen and charisma at the onset of his career. Kellerman (2009) summarizes the sentiment that Barack Obama embodied what Max Weber, a famous twentieth-century sociologist, called "charismatic authority." This kind of leadership is based on the leader's personality and impact on the followers. This leadership is the opposite of traditional authority related to position. Kellerman describes charismatic leadership as being similar to a religious experience.

For me, Obama's run for president was spiritual. At the time, I was in awe that this Black man reflected what my son could become. When I saw the possibility of Obama, who was half white and half Black American, becoming president, I also saw what my Ghanian and African American two-year-old could be. I followed him religiously. At the time, my faculty mentor often took me to lunch to discuss my progress. As my elder, he often talked with me about current politics. He had seen many election cycles but did not believe Obama would be elected as a Black man. We bet that if Obama was elected, I could pick wherever I wanted to go for lunch in Chapel Hill. He obliged, and I ended up at a fancy restaurant for lunch after the election!

In addition to Obama's extraordinary charisma, his grassroots mobilization took everyone by surprise. Aaker and Chang (2009) outline how Obama's campaign used the inception of social media and other technology in ways that had never been done before. The campaign team used social media platforms like Facebook, Twitter, and YouTube to galvanize support and mobilize new voters. An unintended consequence of using these platforms created cross-cultural connections that spanned across multiple identities. This approach led to record-breaking fundraising efforts across donors from across the spectrum.

THINGS OUTSIDE OF HIS CONTROL

However, several factors outside the candidate's control can lead to a successful or failed presidential bid. Some things that were entirely outside of control during the Obama campaign included the economic conditions. During the campaign, Duggan (2023) reports:

> The Great Recession of 2008 to 2009 was the worst economic downturn in the U.S. since the Great Depression. Domestic product declined 4.3%, the unemployment rate doubled to more than 10%, home prices fell roughly 30% at its worst point, the S&P 500 was down 57% from its highs.

As a candidate, there was nothing Obama could have done to avoid this economic disaster. While the world was becoming aware of the dire straits, this situation challenged whoever assumed the presidency. The financial crisis was completely outside of his control.

Moreover, what the opponents would do is outside of the candidate's control. For example, John McCain pulled a stunning move by selecting Sarah Palin as his vice-presidential running mate. This decision immediately gave the GOP momentum as women rallied for a female vice president (Holland, 2008). Obama could not control how the media framed and reported anything. His pastor of many years infamously became the center of controversy because of comments he made in some of his sermons, which incited a great deal of racial discomfort and pushback (Nasaw, 2008). The media portrayed Obama's wife, Michelle, as an angry Black woman or unlikable (Liptak, 2016). At times, the negative media press seemed to impact his polling numbers negatively.

REFLECTION

Reflect on a situation where factors outside of your control impacted your ability to achieve a goal. What did you learn from this experience, and how can you apply these lessons to future challenges?

Another wildcard outside of a candidate's control is voter turnout. Political candidates mobilize their campaigns to get likely and unlikely voters to go to the polls to vote. Political science experts and TV talking heads spend much time predicting voter outcomes. However, voter turnout is outside of the candidate's control. They influence the turnout. President Obama's campaign became masterful in handling its influence.

While President Obama was the unlikely candidate, his campaign team captured what was within their sphere of control and influence to win the presidency successfully. His team responded as best they could to factors outside of their control. Throughout this book, we have examined the complexities associated with actualizing more equitable outcomes in organizations that had not previously done so. Identify what you control and influence to maximize your outcomes, then align them to your actions and resources.

GENDER INCLUSION IMPLEMENTATION SPHERES

During the first couple of months as the equity specialist, I was asked to address gender inclusion within the district. While the term gender inclusion encompasses several actions to protect the rights of individuals regardless of sex or identity, I spent much time supporting the evolution of practice for LGBTQIA+ students and staff. Fueled by the guidance and mentorship of Dr. Colleen Capper during my graduate studies, this issue resonated deeply with me. I felt prepared as I embarked on a journey to provide meaningful change for students and staff who had experienced some challenges related to their gender identity.

Before I did anything, I acquainted myself with how the district handled gender inclusion. I spent time talking with and interacting with personnel across multiple departments. District and school leaders began reaching out to me about individual situations or issues related to trans students. The district lacked uniformity and coherence in how to address the problems of gender equity. It became evident that a comprehensive policy addressing gender inclusion was urgently needed.

Some things were outside my control, making the journey challenging. Poteat and Russell (2013) address the difficulty in changing practices to support LGBTQIA+ students because of how institutionalized and normalized heterosexual relationships are while stigmatizing LGBTQIA+ identities. This environment makes changing the culture and implementing more inclusive practices difficult.

Just as in the broader society, some schools have an inherent resistance to people who are LGBTQIA+. Schools can be a hostile and traumatizing space for them. Kosciw et al. (2016) note that LGBTQIA+ students are often subjected to verbal and physical victimization. As a result, LGBTQIA+ students often have lower academic achievement and higher rates of absenteeism.

Despite facing negative attitudes and staunch resistance, I focused on maximizing what was within my control. I came to this position equipped to understand current best practices from within the context of scholarship. During graduate school, I learned about the negative impact of non-supportive school environments on LGBTQIA+ students. While in the academy, I published an empirical case study on a school principal who positively addressed the needs of LGBTQIA+ students at a high school with an arts focus (Reed & Johnson, 2010). She discussed how she reconciled her long-standing religious beliefs by supporting students regardless of their identities and/or orientation. I used my strength in scholarship to undergird the necessary shifts in policy and practice. I also had a sharp equity intern with a degree in Women's Studies. In addition to being versed in broad gender inclusion issues, she led the research about what best practice guidance existed in other districts.

I enlisted preexisting advocates to champion the work needed to codify gender equity. Several community activist organizations and district teacher advocates had already been working for years to raise awareness and provide advocacy to change policies and practices to align with contemporary best practices for gender inclusion. I created a network with these individuals and amplified their voices. I shared existing qualitative data to underscore the significance of change. Using the actual student quotes to share their negative experiences in some schools and classrooms became a powerful tool to influence staff perceptions. Armed with tenacity and resilience, I confronted resistance head-on, challenging misconceptions and championing equity.

I did not approve the final revision and how it would be implemented. However, I had a sphere of influence and used the influence of the organization's leadership. While there were many contrary and challenging attitudes about gender inclusion, a pivotal moment arose when the superintendent sought my input on shaping the district's policies. She understood the importance and critical nature of providing gender equity and support to students and staff. I pledged to be an advocate for best practices. Using the best practices knowledge I had and the research regarding policies from other districts, I was able to influence and inform her decision-making. I embraced the responsibility to champion inclusivity. Leveraging the superintendent's support, I invoked her endorsement to reinforce the urgency of the cause. I navigated internal dynamics by aligning with her vision and propelled the agenda forward.

Ultimately, the school board of directors passed a revision to the district nondiscrimination policy and directed that district-wide training be provided to understand the new policy and practices. Despite progress, challenges persist. However, the district has since created an infrastructure with a new department and committed resources to support students when challenges arise.

LEAD WITH ICE-T TO CREATE WIN-WINS

Chapter 1 outlined how identity, context, experience, and timing (ICE-T) influence your ability to make equitable decisions. To recap, the "I" is for identity. The "C" is for the context in which you do your work or need to make equity decisions. The "E" represents your experiences due to your identity and context. And the "T" is for timing. You should be constantly aware of the timing in making crucial decisions that will hopefully lead to more equitable outcomes.

Using ICE-T is a powerful tool for becoming a true ally for marginalized individuals or groups. Genuine allyship refers to actively supporting and advocating for marginalized individuals or groups in ways that empower them and promote equity and justice. It involves recognizing your privilege and using it to amplify the voices of those who are often silenced or oppressed. Positive allyship involves actively supporting marginalized individuals or groups, using privilege to amplify voices, educating yourself and others, taking action, challenging discrimination, and centering marginalized voices. For example, allies may amplify LGBTQIA+ voices, educate others about systemic oppression, participate in protests, challenge discriminatory behavior, and ensure diverse perspectives are heard in discussions.

In contrast, chapter 3 outlines the Light Gray Phase with one of its identifiers described as performative allyship. To recap, performative allyship is superficial support for marginalized groups without genuine action. It involves vocalized solidarity for personal gain or to avoid scrutiny. Examples include posting on social media without addressing injustice in real life. From a work perspective, organizations may issue shallow public statements without addressing inequities. This term highlights the importance of genuine, sustained action in allyship efforts rather than merely "talking the talk" without "walking the walk."

As much as we want to believe that everyone wants to do what is just or right according to what we think should be done, that is not always the case. Sometimes, it could be more challenging to advocate when you have shared identities with those you are advocating for. Throughout my life, I have found that it is not always well received when I have spoken up for other people of color. In many cases, when non-Black people spoke on my behalf, it surprisingly was received better. Similarly, in my work for gender inclusion, I often found that people seem to be more receptive to things that I, as a cisgender woman, would say. As a Black woman, I shared upbringings with many other people of color around issues of gender identity and orientation. I understood their reluctance and resistance to new ways of thinking about best practices for gender identity. As I facilitated training, I could speak about my experiences, making new understandings about best practices and acceptance of others.

REFLECTION

What are some examples in your life or work where the T (timing) in ICE-T was outside of your control? How did the timing impact your ability to achieve your goals, and how did you navigate those challenges?

SHE DIDN'T HAVE TO, BUT SHE DID

During my three years as the district equity administrator, I worked with several school leaders. One that left an indelible mark on me was Principal Bain. She was a champion of equity and led a popular French-language magnet specialty city school with a steadfast commitment to ensuring every student had an equal shot at success. Amidst the urban landscape, the school served as a beacon of opportunity for families from diverse backgrounds, drawing students across the district and even the surrounding more affluent suburbs through open enrollment.

While this prestigious public school had high demand and high enrollment, Principal Bain was unsettled by the glaring disparities in student achievement, particularly among students of color, specifically Black boys. Principal Bain was determined to do something about these extreme gaps. Without wavering, she took this challenge head-on.

Because the disparities were related to race, she recognized a need to address race. Bain rallied her staff and collaborated with a district team to embark on a book study by Glenn Singleton (2022) on *Courageous Conversations About Race*. Bain facilitated difficult discussions to foster understanding and empathy among her predominantly white staff.

Once the staff knew the equity direction, Principal Bain redirected the school's vision by inserting language about setting high expectations for all students regardless of their gender, race, or socioeconomic background. Leveraging her shared white identity with many of her staff, Bain engaged in conversations aimed at shifting their teaching practices to serve students of color better. Capitalizing on the school's excellent reputation, she paralleled the importance of equity and cultural responsiveness. This reshaping was well within her sphere of influence and control. She invested her school budget in bringing in speakers who illuminated the systemic barriers faced by students of color in the community, illustrating the urgency of their collective mission.

To match the school's diverse racial demographics, Principal Bain encouraged her staff to incorporate French culture from across the African diaspora. Black students became more interested in the content, increasing academic engagement. With her concerted efforts and expectations, students began to thrive academically and socially with the support of a supportive school culture that valued and centered their identities and cultural assets.

CREATE WRITTEN ACCOUNTABILITY

School districts, companies, hospitals, governmental agencies, and other bureaucracies follow policies and procedures. Rules govern most organizations. I am a member of a consulting cooperative. While we try to operate more collaboratively and collectively, we still have policies, procedures, and regulations. What is most interesting is that we have had some challenging situations when we have not had the appropriate rules and procedures in place. Rules, policies, and procedures dictate how the organization is run, what people can and cannot do, and what they must do. Important things become codified in the organization. Similarly, concerning equity in an organization, policies, procedures, and practices must be codified to get people to rise to the expectations. Given that, it is essential to ensure policies exist.

In the early 2000s, as a new assistant principal, I attended a leadership professional development session with the late Dr. Lorraine Monroe, a vibrant educational leader who founded Harlem's Frederick Douglass Academy. Her exciting leadership was featured on *60 Minutes*. She told colorful stories of how she transformed the educational experiences for numerous students in Harlem, NY. What stuck with me most from her professional development session was that you must "inspect what you expect." That means that you need to have the expectations written down or codified. Otherwise, you will not see what you have espoused to be important.

For example, if you expect teachers to be culturally responsive to students in their instruction, they must know what it means and the expectations. Furthermore, it must be part of the evaluation system. If not, talk about equity and being culturally responsive are disregarded as rhetoric. If it is not written, it will not be respected and executed.

CREATING AN EQUITY POLICY

When I began in the equity position, I spent much time making sure that people understood what equity meant. This meant helping people understand equity from a broad sense and how it differs from equality. For leaders who allowed, I worked with their staff to examine how decisions were made and where the resources were going. We discussed what it meant to shift toward more equitable behavior in the department. These leaders also wanted to make sure that their staff understood what equity meant and how it impacted what they do daily.

Additionally, the superintendent understood that while equity was the new buzzword, an equity policy needed to shift the district's thinking, disposition, and actions. With that, she had my chief and me work with departments and stakeholders across the district to actualize a policy to codify the concept of equity. The school board of directors was also on board with the concept of an equity policy, as during that time, the more progressive districts like Oakland Unified School District had had an equity policy in place for many years. The equity intern and I researched other districts' equity policies and structures. We set out to educate and engage with stakeholders at all levels. We talked to students, teachers, principals, specialized services, the teachers' union, community partners, and many others.

We had difficult conversations with the district parent group. Most parents who attended these monthly meetings regularly had students who attended the better-resourced specialty schools. When I was invited to share the concept of equity with them, it was initially received poorly. Many viewed what I was saying as the district taking their children's resources and giving them to other students. In theory, that could be an option, but the point was that there were several ways that resources could be shifted to support students who needed more. Ultimately, after conversations with their parent leadership team, I revisited the group, and they agreed.

REFLECTION

What policies in your work setting have the most impact on your daily tasks or decision-making? How do these policies influence equity, control, or the distribution of resources?

END-OF-CHAPTER CONSIDERATIONS: LEN LEANS INTO EQUITY

Mr. Leonard "Len" Griffin directs a large school district's community service outreach department. He oversees services supporting about twenty-five community schools out of approximately one hundred fifty total schools. He also oversees before and after-school care and citywide recreational sports. Len's ICE-T is that he is a middle-aged white man who has worked his entire career in the district where he serves as senior director. He started working as a physical education teacher in the district but became interested in services supporting students' extracurricular and other whole-life needs. He began as a supervisor of recreational athletics. Then, Len moved into a manager role and secured the senior director of community, from which he plans to retire in the next few years.

Using what is within his sphere of control, Len has successfully leveraged several partnerships because the Department of Community Service Outreach serves the entire city beyond the district. Under his direction, many positive changes have contributed to increased equity across the city. One major accomplishment from Len's leadership was developing an equity formula to determine what city playgrounds should be renovated. The formula considers the neighborhood's racial makeup, average home income, age, and access to grocery and retail stores. The formula also considered the demographics and needs of the local schools within a ten-mile radius. This formula was used to prioritize which playgrounds were renovated. As a result of this strategy and process, there are more safe outdoor play spaces in some of the city's most disinvested areas.

The district where Len works has prioritized equity. However, there were few resources for the leadership to understand how to identify inequities and create strategies to fix them. Len used his sphere of control and budget to attend equity-based community resource conferences for leaders. He also joined online equity leadership networks to learn best practices in educational community services.

Len also leaned into expressing his equitable mindset expectations among his department's leadership team by directly discussing it in their meetings. Although Len needed to completely understand what was required to become a more equitable department, he knew much work was needed to serve their students and families more equitably. Most of the managers were other white men like him. Most of them had not seen how their identities had garnered privilege. Since the team had been mostly recognized for their good work in the district and community, they rested on their laurels of being a high-performing department.

Previously, their department always had a surplus at the end of the year. Their work has always garnered favor from the superintendent, the senior cabinet, and the district communication department because they have always generated positive press for the district. When Len got his team together to discuss how they needed to focus on equity, his team pushed back. After all, they did not understand the need to shift focus because they were doing so well. Len ensured that his team experienced professional learning on equitable practices in community services and recreation. He brought information from the national organizations that addressed what is equitable in their field. He also sent a few staff members to community equity conferences. The team reconvened in a few months and decided to make some changes within their department.

EQUITY CHALLENGES AND SOLUTIONS IN COMMUNITY OUTREACH

For example, the community outreach department always set aside funding for district students and community members who needed financial assistance to enroll in programs. However, the department did not actively advertise the funds to those who needed grants or free enrollment. After the culturally responsive professional development, the membership team intensified their advertisement strategies to ensure that all the financial assistance was used to increase participation for students or community members who might not otherwise participate. In addition, the community outreach department used an equity lens to create a phased renovation strategy for community spaces that prioritized playgrounds and community centers in lower-income neighborhoods. These equitable shifts ultimately increased student and community engagement in areas that could most benefit from the community outreach resources.

Once Len got his leadership team on board, he knew he had to provide professional development to the rest of the staff. To do that, he contacted Dr. Cecilia Torres, the district's new equity administrator. Len had been involved in training with her. Dr. Torres was tasked to lead a book study on equity with the senior team and their direct reports. Before the book study began, Dr. Torres asked for volunteers from the district leadership team to facilitate the book sessions. Len immediately volunteered to co-facilitate the book study so that he could learn more about equity through his conversations and preparations with Dr. Torres. He didn't have to do it, but he did! After the book study was successfully facilitated, Len contacted the equity administrator and asked her to join his department leadership team in discussions about equity for their department.

In the initial meeting, Len and the managers were excited to begin working with the equity administrator. Len, his leadership team, and the equity administrator discussed what they learned through their department's research on equity. The equity administrator began to share some ideas about ways the department could explore what equity means in the various areas represented.

After conducting departmental research, the community outreach staff identified two key staffing areas for improvement. First, they recognized the need to increase bilingual staff recruitment to better serve Spanish-speaking community centers. Second, after analyzing feedback, the department leaders found that many part-time sports referees had negative perceptions about working in certain areas of the city. Since referees were allowed to select their officiating locations, these perceptions influenced staffing patterns, creating gaps in coverage for some sites. The department leaders opted to create professional development for the part-time referees. The training focus was to address negative perceptions of program participants and provide relationship-building strategies to support officiating regardless of their assigned location.

Len maximized all the training resources the district had offered. He made sure that he often connected with Dr. Torres to be a thought partner and resource to the work the department aspired to do. He attended additional trainings that Dr. Torres invited him to and advocated for his staff to participate when the opportunity arose. In addition, within his sphere of influence, he made sure that he set aside professional learning time for the department to explore what equity meant. He also required that his managers participate in the decision-making around how equity was implemented in the department. He created spaces where all areas would be brought to the table by establishing professional development leaders for each department area.

WORKING THROUGH DISCOMFORT TO ACHIEVE EQUITY

Even though Len and his professional learning team experienced some challenges while facilitating some professional development, he persisted. After one of the professional learning experiences, a few of his white male managers expressed that they were extremely uncomfortable with some of the topics addressed in the training. During one of the earlier professional development sessions, the facilitator wanted everyone to understand how some identities had advantages over others. The managers reflected on how their gender and race may have led to certain privileges. In their session feedback, they expressed discomfort and concern as they grappled with this revelation. Some even talked directly to Len about their discontent.

Len continued the equity sessions, adding one-on-one support and reinforcing group norms to foster engagement and growth. Instead of weakening or stopping the equity content altogether, Len drew on his ICE-T to address their concerns. He shared with the managers how uncomfortable he initially felt coming to a similar realization. However, he discussed how he slowed down and listened to the professional experiences of people of color and women. He learned that some had been qualified or overqualified for specific promotions but did not receive them. Through one-on-one conversations, Len shared how he used his identity to lift equity for others without a voice. The training facilitators also addressed the challenges by reminding the team of the group norms that identified growth as something that could come from being uncomfortable hearing other perspectives.

After three years of stretching and pushing his staff, Len codified and validated the equity work by allocating a position for an equity point person. He hired someone to provide equity technical support to all areas in the department. By maximizing his spheres of control, he hopes this progress will be sustainable even after he retires.

Questions to Consider

1. Given the issues of equity that you are trying to solve in your work context:
   a. What are things within your control?
   b. What are things within your sphere of influence?
   c. What are things outside of our control? How will you mitigate or work around those things?
2. Given your ICE-T, in what ways do you consider yourself to be an ally to marginalized people or groups?
   a. Describe a situation where you used your ICE-T to be an ally.
   b. What are some ways that you can use your ICE-T to advance equitable outcomes?
   c. How can you use your ICE-T?
3. What infrastructures currently exist to support the advancement of equity within your current work context?
   a. Describe the professional development or learning that consistently supports learning best culturally responsive practices to address the diverse needs of those you serve.
   b. If no professional development or learning exists, what is needed to ensure that the organization knows best practices?
4. Where are equitable practices written? If there is no written accountability, what policies or procedures does your organization need?

CHAPTER 6

The Black Phase

Historically, the color black has been equated or associated with bad, sad, menacing, or negative feelings and emotions. In 1979, researcher Longshore (1979) used a simple word-pair scale (beautiful-ugly, nice-awful, clean-dirty, etc.) to demonstrate that adult white individuals responded more negatively to the color black as compared to red, white, yellow, and brown, and that those white individuals held similar associations when asked to respond to terms like "White people" and "Black people." Black individuals, on the other hand, held significantly more positive attitudes toward both the color "black" and "black people."

In many movies or books, villainous characters wear ominous black clothing and seek to accomplish evil deeds, a trend as visible in modern Disney films as it is in the works of Shakespeare. Numerous studies have demonstrated that people carry such connotations into their daily lives, even when they are very young. One of the most famous studies of this kind was conducted by Drs. Kenneth and Mamie Clark and published in 1947 under the title "Racial Identification and Preference in Negro Children." Often referred to as the "Dolls Test," the results of this study showed that children as young as three have color and racial preferences that echo the black and white preferences demonstrated in Longshore. The Clarks' research was so powerful that it provided the psychological basis to strike down the "separate but equal" doctrine in the landmark *Brown v. Board of Education* case of 1954.

In the EEC, these negative notions are flipped on their head. To describe the Black Phase, I borrow from a positive business term: to be "in the black." This is a phrase that indicates profit and progress. It stems from accounting practice where profits are displayed in reports using black ink or text, and losses are displayed in red. In this sense, the Black Phase of EEC embodies taking a solid, clear stand on issues of inequality and inequity that will make a positive difference and engender progress. The Black Phase aims to produce equitable outcomes in systems or organizations that are sustainable beyond a specific leader or leadership group. The three Black Phase identifiers are described as the following:

1. Aspiration – The enduring ideas about equity and justice
2. Movements – The actions that bring about equity and justice
3. Comprehensive Codification – The foundational pillars that provide equity and justice

The Black Phase is not limited to these three identifiers. Yet, these three describe the foundation that keeps the quest for equity and justice alive and well.

1. ASPIRATION

Justice is not easily defined, but the lack of it is palpable, and its effects undeniable. However, in *The Theory of Justice*, Rawls (1971), an American political and moral philosopher who spent most of his career at Harvard, defines justice. He describes two principles. The first is the "liberty principle," which calls for basic equal liberties for all. The second is the "difference principle," which permits inequalities only if they benefit the least advantaged members of society. Sen (2009), an Indian economist, philosopher, and author, provides critique of Rawl's work, mostly pointing out that his theory is abstract and idealistic. In *The Idea of Justice*, Sen iterates that the focus should be on real inequalities and how to improve the lived experiences of those who experience it. In practical terms, instead of ensuring an equity statement is in the district vision, it would be prudent to have specific language demonstrating how equitable principles are carried out to justly serve the needs of those who need it most.

The district should use intentional language to express its commitment to equity. For instance, it can include a clear statement describing how decisions are made through an equity lens. A potential vision statement could read, "We use data to identify inequities and guide decisions that promote equitable outcomes for all students." Similarly, the district should articulate its dedication to a culturally responsive curriculum. A specific example might state, "We provide a curriculum that reflects the diversity of our community."

So many things are attached to justice. My doctoral program at the University of Wisconsin-Madison centered on social justice educational leadership. There is also environmental justice, food justice, medical ethics justice, land justice, and more. In each area, people organize around what they see necessary to achieve justice or equity, creating movements toward these goals.

REFLECTION

How do you define justice, particularly in the context of equity? How does this definition shape your decisions and practices within your personal life and work environment?

While those who inflict oppression may believe the imbalance benefits them, it erodes their humanity. Decoteau Irby discusses the impact of white supremacy on those who perpetuate racism and oppression, asserting that the most devastating part of racism is "its adverse impacts on our ability to be our best human selves (Irby, 2021, p. 57)." When one group consistently denigrates and oppresses another, neither group achieves true humanity. Aspiration for justice is the common thread that drives the pursuit of a more humane and equitable world.

Before justice can occur, an aspiration for it must exist. Dr. King said, "I have a dream," signifying that his vision of justice was not yet a reality. He envisioned the end of Jim Crow and the inequalities present during that time. There is often a wide gap between the grand ideas of equity and justice and the current reality. Aspirations fuel and inspire the pursuit to develop actionable plans. To reiterate, policies, practices, and procedures don't change the practice: People do! Hence, people need to nurture their aspirations for justice to move forward.

Bettina Love (2019), author of *We Want to Do More Than Survive: Abolitionist Teaching and the Pursuit of Educational Freedom*, describes this aspiration as the "theoretical imagination." Love draws from Maxine Greene, an influential education author and advocate, who encouraged the use of imagination to help overcome limitations and promote freedom in education. Love states:

> Arguably, abolitionists' greatest tools against injustice were their imaginations. Their imaginations fueled their resistance. Imagining being free, imagining reading, imagining loving the love of your life, imagining your children being free, imagining life and not death, imagining seeing the world, and imagining Freedom. These Freedom dreams drive out apathy, and the Quest for Freedom becomes an internal desire necessary to preserve humanity (Love, 2019, p. 102).

Imagining alternate scenarios to the current reality is crucial in defeating pessimism and apathy in education. This aspiration for justice drives us to envision and create better futures.

I am not sure if my enslaved ancestors believed their descendants would one day be free in the same land where they were enslaved. However, I have read enough accounts and seen enough movies to know that enslaved Black people surely aspired for freedom. They risked their lives by running away. White allies aligned their aspirations and actions to advocate for a more just country, culminating in the 13th Amendment to end slavery in the US.

As I prepare to send my son to college, I *really* want him to have an experience free from the dangers of being young, Black, and male. I am always hopeful that my son will not endure the horrors I have seen or heard in the media, social media, and first-person accounts. My aspiration is for my son to live free and in a world where young Black men do not worry about a traffic stop encounter ending in a beating or death. Sometimes, this aspiration is strong, and other times it sits still in the pit of my stomach. Despite this underlying threat, countless other mothers of Black men and I continue to nurture and celebrate our sons, hoping for a day when we don't excessively worry about them. Whether it is freedom from being a slave or freedom from the threat of harm, our imagination allows us to keep aspiring for a more just world.

Throughout this book, I have highlighted many who have enacted change. Their persistent aspirations for change kept them fueled to do the work in the face of resistance. Similarly, you work toward equity today, understanding what creates inequitable environments for individuals and groups, but still embracing the challenge with the aspiration for justice in mind.

PUBLIC EDUCATION ASPIRATIONS:

From the mid-nineteenth century to the early twentieth century, two major aspirations persisted in public education: (1) a desire for quality education and (2) equal access to education. During that time, philosophers and advocates espoused aspirational ideas about what should be taught, who should teach it, and who could receive it. These philosophers and advocates all held similar aspirations. But they differed in their approaches to obtaining quality education and access to it.

QUALITY

Before the nineteenth century, educational practices in the US were inconsistent and lacked formal regulation. Tyack (1974) notes that education was not systemically regulated. The curriculum was rudimentary and focused on basic literacy, math computation, and religious instruction, though some students were allowed to participate in apprenticeships instead. During this time, some schools were led by religious idealogues who provided a biased perspective in education that was not to be challenged (Cremin, 1980; Spring, 2024). Other education was provided in homes by self-taught teachers resulting in various levels of training and student instruction.

Moreover, changes in education during the nineteenth and early twentieth centuries were required to meet the evolving socioeconomic landscape. As social reforms such as abolition, women's rights, and the temperance movement arose, a need for understanding societal improvement arose (Reese, 2011)—democratic ideals required informed citizens to sustain a healthy democracy (Cremin, 1980). With increased industry, a more literate and skilled worker was required to perform factory jobs (Rury, 2005). With this new industry, there was a need to address the emerging poverty and crime in cities. (Tyack, 1974).

For these reasons, philosophers, educators, and advocates articulated specific aspirations for improved quality and access. Horace Mann advocated for free, nonsectarian schools with well-trained teachers. Born in 1796, he was a leading advocate for education and became the first Secretary of the Massachusetts State Board of Education (1837–1848). Mann believed teaching should be professionalized with formal training programs to provide standard pedagogy. Additionally, in the nineteenth century, Beecher (1835) also believed it was important to have qualified teachers teaching students and that women could do so as an extension of their nurturing nature. Beecher (n.d.), a writer, advocate for kindergarten, and a strong proponent for teacher training programs, advocated for women to become teachers. At the time, women were not seen as being suitable to teach. She promoted the teaching profession as a respectable career for women at a time when women working outside of the home was generally not accepted.

During the early twentieth century, John Dewey and other educational philosophers spearheaded the Progressive Education Movement. This movement emphasized and advocated for democratic citizenship, experiential learning, and critical thinking for children. Dewey aspired to bring the benefits of education to more people and to expand the curricular content to be student-centered and inclusive of their experiences (Dewey, 1916/2024). This was a major departure for his time because education was widely viewed as merely a transfer of knowledge from teacher to student. Furthermore, it was radical to use education as a tool to nurture democratic ideas.

Booker T. Washington also aspired for Black people to have standardized training that provided practical skills in various fields such as agriculture and carpentry (Graham, 2005). While he differed from other popular Black contemporaries of the time like W.E.B. Dubois, he garnered influence and resources for K-12 education at Tuskegee Normal and Industrial Institute, which he founded. His approach influenced K-12 education at Tuskegee by integrating vocational training with academics, preparing students for skilled labor and personal development.

Mary McLeod Bethune was born in 1875 and was the daughter of former slaves (Bethune, 2002). She desired a better curriculum for Black students and believed that they should have access to both well-rounded liberal arts and vocational experiences (Hanson, 2003). McLeod, herself, was aspirational and inspirational for many as a Black highly educated woman who started the Daytona Normal and Industrial Institute for Negro Girls. The school later became Bethune-Cookman University. She also served as an advisor to President Franklin D. Roosevelt and was part of his "Black Cabinet."

By the mid-twentieth century, during the civil rights era, people aspired to a desegregated school. These ideas were sparked at times when there was no public school system, women were not encouraged to teach or have professions outside of the home, and children went to segregated schools. However, aspiration spurred change in compensatory education for grades kindergarten to twelfth grade, a profession that is now dominated by women, and desegregated schools.

ACCESS

Historically, access to education was limited, especially for marginalized groups. Malcolm X said, "Education is the passport to the future." However, like most things in the US, marginalized people were denied their passports. Tyack (1974) found that education in the US was accessible mostly to the wealthy. As already discussed in this book, Black people were denied access to education (see page 68). Throughout US history, other racial and ethnic groups were also denied access to education or offered alternate types of education. Native Americans were forced to assimilation boarding schools where they were taught to abandon their traditions and adopt white culture (Churchill, 2004). In many states, Hispanic/Latinx children faced segregated and less equipped schools (Gándara & Contreras, 2009). During the Japanese internment, Asian American students were denied access to education (Tunnell & Chilcoat, 2011). Bethune believed that educating all races would uplift the entire country. (Bethune, 2002).

Women also have not had equal access to education (Kaestle, 1983). This unequal and unjust condition of widespread educational access created an aspiration for change. In the face of resistance, the pursuit of educational access festered throughout each group that was denied. Overtime, those marginalized by lack of access have been driven by their aspirations to access education.

2. MOVEMENTS

We live in a binary era where people stand on two sides of the fence on how to address the inequities and imbalances that exist in our communities, country, and across the globe. However, when we achieve more balance, there is more justice. Frederick Douglass said, "Where justice is denied, where poverty is enforced, where ignorance prevails, and where any one class is made to feel that society is an organized conspiracy to oppress, rob, and degrade them, neither persons nor property will be safe." So many things have been attached to justice. My doctoral program at the University of Wisconsin–Madison was centered on social justice leadership for educators. But there is also environmental justice, food justice, medical ethics justice, land justice, and so forth. In the Black Phase, people organize around what they see as necessary to achieve justice or equity. This becomes a movement.

Gage (2018) of the *New York Times* believes that movements have changed. Movements, including and before the Civil Rights movements, were significantly different. For example, the 1963 March on Washington was a pinnacle display of a powerful coalition that symbolized resistance to the Jim Crow era. However, today, similar large events are usually viewed as the beginning of something. Seemingly, it has been easier to begin or mobilize a movement due to social media. On the other hand, sustaining momentum and translating movements into actual change is more challenging. Modern movements typically are more individualistic without emphasis on institutional change.

WHAT MAKES A MOVEMENT SUCCESSFUL?

Milliken (2021) summarized several Northwestern University scholars' views on how movements are started. She says that movements involve mobilizing people around a shared issue, organizing effectively, maintaining public relevance, and employing diverse tactics to create meaningful change. Successful movements are typically marked by several factors that lead to successfully bringing about change. Satell (2016) outlines these successful attributes.

1. A clear purpose must be established that is well-defined, gives direction, and rallies supporters.
2. The movement must provide principle and values training for activists to stay disciplined and on track.
3. While large gatherings attract attention, networks of smaller groups must be built to ensure the movement's interconnectedness.
4. Movement activities must be strategically planned in a sequential order that builds support and momentum.
5. The movement must appeal to people beyond the core activists and supporters to expand its influence.
6. There must be personal interactions with stakeholders and decision-makers to change minds and find common interests.
7. Find ways to allow opposition sides to feel like they have gained instead of only destroying them.

Satell offers a stark contrast between a successful and a failed movement using the examples of the 1998 Otpor Movement in Serbia and the 2011 Occupy Wall Street movement in the

US. The goal of the Serbian youth was to overthrow Slobodan Milošević's regime because of the authoritarian rule, economic failures, corruption, war crimes, and human rights abuse. They succeeded in 2000 by utilizing the key attributes of successful movements through disciplined, nonviolent resistance and organizing. They maintained a clear purpose and instituted systemic ways to train protesters. They also built coalitions of smaller groups within the movement.

In contrast, Occupy Wall Street experienced an anticlimactic campaign. The group started protests in Zuccotti Park in Manhattan. They protested corporate influence on US politics and economic disparities. This movement spread to other cities and countries quickly. However, it was short-lived because the goals were not clear. There were several, vague grievances, but no specific demands or solutions were offered. There was no specific training for those involved in protesting. With no training and decentralized leadership, the movement faded without tangible results other than heightened attention to disparities only after a few months.

The Occupy movement didn't provide specific demands or solutions. Unlike Otpor, Occupy did not emphasize training or discipline, and its decentralized structure, while inclusive, made it difficult to maintain focus or achieve concrete outcomes. The movement faded within months, achieving limited tangible results despite its initial momentum. With clear focus and strategy, the Otpor was able to move a regime out. On the other hand, a lack of clarity and organization were the key barriers to the Occupy Wall Street movement.

MOVEMENTS IN EDUCATION

A public education system was established due to aspirations for a higher-quality education and increased access to American schools. The aspirations were having quality education with broader access. However, several movements brought about a change that created what we know as public education today. Public schools aim to ensure everyone has access to education regardless of class, race, religion, gender, ability, or other identities. Advocates, leaders, and groups created movements to actualize the aspiration to create public schools.

In the nineteenth century, Horace Mann led the Common School Movement (Cremin, 1980; Spring, 2024). Kaestle (1983) says that Mann built a coalition of reformers who saw education as a means to improve society. Other collaborators included industrialists who wanted to ensure an educated workforce. Protestant religious leaders supported the Common Schools movement because it included moral education. Political leaders also believed that providing education would strengthen democracy. These smaller groups created the change by capitalizing on the win-win message that society would be more educated to participate in democracy. Parents, regardless of income, could provide education for their children. Businesses gained a more educated workforce.

During the early twentieth century, John Dewey and other educational philosophers spearheaded the Progressive Education Movement. This movement emphasized and advocated for democratic citizenship, experiential learning, and critical thinking for children. Dewey gained momentum from his Chicago Laboratory Schools, where he experimented with many of his ideas and aspirations. He published and discussed the results, which persuaded people to accept them.

By the mid-twentieth century, during the civil rights era, aspirations grew for better conditions for Black people in schools, which included desegregation after years of oppressive Jim Crow laws allowed poor quality for Black children and segregated schools. Leaders like Dorothy Height used her leadership skills to improve the education of Black students. Dorothy Height used a combination of grassroots and national advocacy to spur changes in desegregating education (Height, 2009). She led the National Council of Negro Women (NCNW), which advocated for school reform and better conditions for Black students.

Legal leaders like Thurgood Marshall and Constance Baker Motley were prominent civil rights lawyers who specifically focused on dismantling segregation in the US. It is well known that Thurgood Marshall later became the first Black Supreme Court Justice. Baker Motley, who served as Marshall's law clerk, was the only woman on the legal defense team for the NAACP (Brown-Nagin, 2022). She served as defense counsel for Dr. Martin Luther King. Baker Motley was a law clerk with Marshall in *Brown v. The Board of Education*. She was also the first Black woman appointed as a federal judge.

In conclusion, multiple movements and leaders have started and sustained efforts to advance public education. The Common School Movement united reformers, industrialists, and religious leaders on teacher training and free access to education. The Progressive Education Movement promoted democratic values and experiential learning. The Civil Rights Movement developed and strategically executed a case for educational equity and desegregation. In these movements, leaders emerged who could rally people within and outside of the cause to influence change. These leaders shared clear messaging about the need for change and capitalized on coalitions to unite multiple stakeholders for the cause. Their strategic alliances and focused messages were vital to realizing education as a universal right and a force for societal progress.

3. COMPREHENSIVE CODIFICATION

After aspirations have been turned into a movement, comprehensive codification changes the trajectory of justice. In chapter 5, written accountability was discussed. This is where equity accountability is built within the system or organizations. Comprehensive codifications are constitutional rights, amendments, federal legislation, and court cases that provide a standard of equality for all people. They have a wide-ranging impact on the broader society. Throughout this book, we have explored how different historical and contemporary people have fought for the rights of those in society who have fought for marginalized individuals or groups. Chapter 1 examined the contradictions in the US Constitution, which states that "all men are created equal." As much as the founding fathers may have wanted to believe this, it is telling that they wrote it in the Constitution. The founders knew that inequalities and inequities existed, needed to be called out, and had some official codification to ensure this would be the federal expectation. We use comprehensive codifications as the foundation to undergird our work within our sphere of influence and control.

In chapter 5, in the Dark Gray Phase, organizations ensure accountability is written within the policies and procedures. To review, accountability codification means putting specific rules or laws in place to ensure equitable expectations are met. In the Black Phase, comprehensive codifications are large-scale decisions and/or actions that lead to justice for marginalized people and/or groups.

Most high school civic courses cover the gist of comprehensive codification, which outlines the pillars of how the US democracy is supposed to operate. These courses typically have information about government structure, the constitution, the rights and freedoms afforded to all citizens, voting, public policy, and global positionality and perspectives. As a nation, the US has embraced federalism, a system in which power is shared between national, state, and sometimes local governments. Radin and Boase (2000) explain that while the US has accepted power-sharing arrangements, it intentionally operates with fragmented powers to prevent authority concentration. This fragmentation occurs horizontally and vertically, with separate institutions and powers distributed across different levels of government. In a federalist system, power is shared between the national and local governments, whereas the unitary system empowers the national government with local states at its discretion (Elazar, 1987). The federal system can cause disparities between states and cities within the nation. As a result of the interplay between the different levels, policies evolve over time versus systemic planning.

In the US, our Constitution is the foundational legal document that codifies the federal government structure. It defines the differentiated powers and protects the rights of the citizens. The main pillars of federal comprehensive codification are:

> **The United States Constitution:** This key document was ratified in 1789 and is the ultimate law of the land. The Constitution mandates three branches of government including legislative, executive, and judicial. It provides limitation and oversight for each of the equal branches. Fundamental rights are protected through comprehensive amendments that clarify the initial intents of the Constitution.
>
> **Bill of Rights:** In 1791, the first ten Constitutional amendments were ratified to guarantee fundamental rights and freedoms in the Bill of Rights. These amendments provided freedom of speech, religion, press, the right to bear arms, protection against unreasonable searches, and the right to a fair trial.

Amendments to the Constitution: There have been additional amendments that are beyond the Bill of Rights that have changed the trajectory for oppressed groups of people in the US. These overarching amendments include the abolition of slavery in the 13th Amendment, the ability to vote regardless of race in the 15th Amendment, and the right of women to vote in the 19th Amendment.

Supreme Court Decisions: Important Supreme Court decisions have also clarified the intent and outcome of the Constitution. These cases have set legal precedents that provide civil rights and the separation of powers. In education, one of the most famous rulings is *Brown v. Board of Education* (1954), which officially ended segregation in public schools. The ruling deemed segregation unconstitutional.

Federal Laws: Congress makes federal laws that are broad-reaching and govern national life, criminal law, immigration, environmental regulations, and civil rights. Checks and balances ensure that these laws are constitutional. The Supreme Court can declare a law unconstitutional.

State Constitutions and Laws: Each state has a constitution and legal structures that are mostly congruent with the federal constitution and framework. These laws oversee various issues, including education, criminal justice systems, health care, and property rights.

COMPREHENSIVE CODIFICATION IN EDUCATION

There have been several comprehensive codifications in education. Some of these comprehensive codifications include but are not limited to the following:

Elementary and Secondary Education Act (ESEA) (US Department of Education, n.d.a.): This law was passed as part of President Lyndon Johnson's "War on Poverty." The goal was to mitigate educational inequalities and provide financial resources for "disadvantaged" children. President Barack Obama reauthorized this act in 2015.

Civil Rights Act of 1964 (US Department of Justice, n.d.): This law prevents discrimination on the basis of race, color, or national origin in all activities that receive federal funding. It was meant to end the segregation that continued even after the 1954 *Brown vs. Board* decision.

Every Student Succeeds Act (ESSA) (US Department of Education, n.d.b.): Under President Barack Obama, the ESSA was signed into law to replace the more restrictive No Child Left Behind Act (NCLB). This act aims to ensure flexibility with state funding but also maintain federal oversight to hold states accountable for equitable services.

Individuals with Disabilities Education Act (IDEA) (US Department of Education, n.d.c.): In 1975, IDEA mandated individualized education plans (IEPs) for qualifying students to receive specialized services and instruction that accommodate their learning disability. This Act has been subsequently reauthorized.

These significant comprehensive codifications have provided advancements for individuals and groups without access to resources and/or opportunities. Many of these advances are central to achieving equity. It is essential to protect these pillars to ensure the protections for those individuals and groups who have not historically had equal access.

NAVIGATING THE COMPLEXITY OF THE BLACK PHASE

The Black Phase, the ultimate picture of equity and justice, is a concept that is challenging to articulate due to the scarcity of sustained examples. If the EEC were to fit into the four categories, the end phase would be the perfect picture of equity and justice. However, the realization of this ideal remains uncertain. As an optimist, I believe in the inherent desire of most individuals to ensure everyone is treated fairly. Yet, the present reality often forces me to adopt a more cautious perspective.

An ongoing battle between our virtues and vices prohibits us from truly reaching a place where all can be treated equally and equitably. While we have lofty ideas of being a “good” society, we struggle to meet the mark due to the human condition. Simply, the human condition is the range of experiences associated with being human. Arendt (2013), philosopher and author of *The Human Condition,* describes it as the things that impact human life, such as birth, death, and the many things that happen in the world and on the earth. How we navigate those experiences causes us to either "do the right thing" or not.

Over time, religious philosophers have tried to make peace with our inherent flaws based on the human condition. The *Bhagavad Gita*, the Hindu scriptures, expresses the inner conflict of a warrior who struggles with going to war. To paraphrase *Bhagavad Gita* (2024, 3:36), the warrior is driven by impulses he does not understand, causing him to act in ways he does not actually approve of. In the *Bible* (n.d.), the Apostle Paul discusses wanting to do right but doing the wrong thing. The *Holy Bible* (n.d., Romans 7:19) says, "For I do not do the good I want to do, but the evil I do not want to do—this I keep on doing." In Surah Al-Isra, the *Qur'an* (2024, 17:11) says, "And humans swiftly pray for evil as they pray for good. For humankind is ever hasty." These statements all explain the complexity of why people do not always "do the right thing." This complex reality of anger, evil, conflict, and struggle makes it difficult to fully flesh out what an ultimate Black Phase should look like.

In chapter 3, we discussed how progress is dialed back when people operate within the White Phase of the continuum. In the Black Phase, individuals and groups work tirelessly to build an equitable infrastructure that creates justice for marginalized people. The Black Phase is the hardest to describe because there are so few examples of sustained equity and justice that I can draw from. If the EEC told a traditional story with a happy ending, then the Black Phase would tell the tale of perfect equity and justice and would provide a way for everyone to realize their goals. But I am unsure that is possible.

As previously mentioned in this chapter, justice can be defined by theory. However, it is more useful to define **actions** that lead to equity and justice. While we have lofty ideas of being a "good" society, we struggle against our human nature. We must acknowledge and face our vulnerabilities to achieve equity and justice. James Baldwin (1963) said, "Love takes off the masks that we fear we cannot live without and know we cannot live within (p. 21)." How we navigate that unveiling leads us to either "do the right thing" or not.

The Black Phase is defined as continuously seeking equity and justice and working to maintain progress for marginalized people and groups in the face of resistance. Those who seek to be more equitable use the Black Phase identifiers to work within their context and sphere of influence to increase equitable practices. When you are in the Black Phase, you build upon the ongoing aspirations that exists for justice, embrace the symbolic movements and events of the past, and use the comprehensive legislation or decisions to impact change. Even if the mark is missed, you must continue to strive to do the work. You must positively reinforce and reiterate actions that will move everyone closer to the equitable outcomes you seek. The goal is to keep pushing through the roadblocks you have learned about in the White and light gray phases so that the victories of the dark gray and Black Phases can become a reality. Continue reinforcing the identifiers in the Dark Gray Phase that move you toward the goal of equity and justice for all. In other words, when you know better, continue to do better.

REFLECTION

In what ways has the "human condition" hindered equity progress in your personal or professional context? How do you personally reconcile the uncertainty in your equity work, and what motivates you to continue striving for better outcomes despite it?

END-OF-CHAPTER CONSIDERATIONS: WHEN DOING THE RIGHT THING GOES WRONG!

Dr. Bianca Simmons, a Black female superintendent, is a leader for equity. Her ICE-T is complex as her identity, context, and experiences are unique and complicated. Over time, her ICE-T influenced what she accomplished to mitigate inequities for the marginalized. She grew up in a well-to-do area in a Midwestern city in the north, where her parents were also educators. Her mother was the CEO of a major textbook company. Dr. Simmons followed in her father's footsteps by becoming a superintendent. Having been immersed in the education sector her whole life, she attended a suburban school district in the Midwest but remained connected to city culture. She participated in various community activities and worshipped at a historically Black Baptist church with a progressive agenda, frequently volunteering and giving back to the metropolitan area.

Despite attending a predominantly white high school in a wealthy suburb, Bianca chose to attend a prominent HBCU in the south where she studied secondary math education. After college, she returned home and worked as a high school math teacher in a large urban school district. Her school had many challenging opportunities and a predominantly Black and Latino student body. For many years, she successfully helped students pass calculus through her culturally responsive approaches and relationship-building.

Over the next ten years, Bianca continued as a classroom teacher while obtaining a master's and doctorate from a prestigious Ivy League school of education. Around the time she received her PhD in educational leadership, she became an assistant principal at her school. After only three years, she became a principal at a school similar to where she taught.

While the student population was diverse and presented many challenging opportunities that other urban schools faced, she used her community-building and nurturing disposition to rally the students and staff to overcome those challenges. After being principal for five years, she was tapped by the district office to be a deputy superintendent. In this role, she monitored the school curriculum and coordinated resources to create district-wide coherence. She also implemented restorative practices, which promote relationship-building, repairing harm, and establishing accountability. The implementation of restorative practices helped improve school culture and climate while significantly reducing disciplinary incidents district-wide. Teachers and administrators found that classroom referrals, out-of-school suspensions and expulsions drastically decreased. Teachers and school principals greatly appreciated her hands-on leadership approach, finding her accessible, personable, and supportive, which increased district morale.

When a superintendent position opened in a mid-large-sized school district in a Midwestern state, an executive search firm reached out to her and encouraged her to apply. After an extensive search, Dr. Simmons was selected to lead the district in spring 2019. Dr. Simmons spent her first ninety days understanding the issues her new school district faced. She engaged with all stakeholders, including students, families, teachers, school leaders, and the community. She carefully reviewed numerous data points and talked to several stakeholders. At the end of the ninety days, she identified several major issues confronting the district.

Dr. Simmons established four improvement goals for her administration. This agenda included addressing the achievement gap, increasing equitable decision-making with district funding and resources, bolstering student well-being and safety, and recruiting and retaining highly qualified teachers. Dr. Simmons and her team hit the ground quickly and worked on each of the goals.

Like the rest of the world, when COVID-19 struck in 2020, Dr. Simmons had to lead her district through a difficult and tumultuous time. The pandemic shutdown exposed issues of inequity for marginalized students in the district. This crisis created a movement across the country to ensure that students had access to technology regardless of their background. Many teachers, now privy to their students' home environments, understood the disparities that had always existed. This situation created an urgent need to align with many of the goals Dr. Simmons put forth when she became superintendent. Those who had always aspired to see changes for marginalized students found their voices amplified.

Dr. Simmons and her administration took advantage of the comprehensive guidelines and recovery funding handed down by the federal government to manage the pandemic crisis. Because she had the confidence of her district, she was able to navigate these trying times more successfully than other similar districts.

Initially, the board was extremely excited and supportive of the changes Dr. Simmons facilitated in the identified areas. As Dr. Simmons began to assemble her administrative team and support, she worked closely with the board to address the crucial issues impacting the school district. Even though, initially, the board supported their newly hired superintendent, by 2022, the honeymoon seemed to be waning. She heard that her initiatives were ruffling the feathers of many teachers and administrators who had been in the district for more than twenty-five years, many of whom were not interested in retiring.

Although Dr. Simmons had an impressive record of building morale among staff and fostering engagement with families and communities, she faced criticism for being too progressive with her changes. Various groups voiced their discontent. Dr. Simmons aimed to implement restorative practices, which had been successful in her previous district. She ensured the district budget allocated sufficient funding for each school to adopt these practices effectively. However, many teachers perceived the restorative practices model as being too lenient on student discipline and refused to participate in the training. They also filed grievances when heavy sanctions were not imposed on students, even though they refused to engage in restorative solutions for challenging behaviors.

Dr. Simmons encouraged teachers to align their curriculum with culturally responsive topics that reflected the district's students of color. Some dismissed cultural responsiveness as "that CRT stuff" and expressed discomfort in discussing its integration. Additionally, veteran curriculum leaders were uncomfortable facilitating professional development on culturally responsive topics such as Black History and LGBTQIA+ issues. The leaders resisted efforts to integrate them into the curriculum and teacher professional development. Dr. Simmons also wanted to ensure that principals' and teachers' data were disaggregated by race, class, disability status, and other marginalized identities. However, the assessment director pushed back over including equitable measurements in evaluating district success.

Some parents misunderstood and complained about the resource realignment taking place in schools. Parents in wealthier areas became disgruntled at the prospect of losing resources, as their schools were well funded. They criticized her leadership style and labeled her as "angry" during meetings about negotiating benefits and conditions for teachers. After a year, members of the community pressured the district to ban books that were being banned in other districts. These books covered progressive topics like police brutality in *The Hate U Give* (Thomas, 2017), racial inequality and slurs in *To Kill a Mockingbird* (Lee, 1960), LGBTQIA+ themes in *Gender Queer: A Memoir* (Kobabe, 2019), and traditional gender roles and women's rights in *The Handmaid's Tale* (Atwood, 1985). Local churches joined in protests to eliminate them from the curriculum and libraries.

Like many districts across the country, Dr. Simmons's district struggled with a teacher shortage. She collaborated with the state Department of Public Instruction to devise creative recruitment measures within state licensing requirements. She also worked with her curriculum chief to ensure new teachers received adequate support through coaching partnerships with the local university. However, some principals opposed the prospect of new teachers who had not been certified in traditional programs in their buildings, and HR professionals disagreed with the new recruitment strategy.

Despite Dr. Simmons and her administrative team achieving improved state standard test scores, better culture and climate data, and overall satisfaction improvement, dissenting voices grew louder. Dr. Simmons was unsure why she had become the target of various groups. Over time, she noticed that these dissenting groups formed a vocal coalition that undermined her work. Despite her immaculate background, documented results, and education from prestigious universities, she was often asked if she was a "DEI hire" or a token. Conversations with some leaders who opposed her often included assumptions about her background and questions about whether she had to work twice as hard because she came from "the hood."

Many of her naysayers failed to recognize her training at one of the best HBCUs and Ivy League institutions. While they acknowledged her ability to articulate theories of restorative practices and innovative ways to reach marginalized students, they insisted on keeping the curriculum basic and free of political ideology. Many leaders opposing her changes did not understand the need for equitable adjustments for students with different gender identities or those needing language acquisition accommodations. When issues of race arose, they often dismissed them with statements like, "I don't see color, I just see people," or "Racism is not as bad as it used to be."

In the spring of 2024, after five years of service, Dr. Bianca Simmons faced the school board's decision to renew her contract. Despite her accomplishments in boosting morale, engaging the community, and improving academic outcomes, the board was under intense pressure from factions opposed to her changes.

During the public meeting where Dr. Simmons's contract renewal was to be considered, hundreds of supporters filled the auditorium in support. Several of the supporters came to the microphone to speak on her behalf. Parents talked about how their child's school had been transformed and how impressed they were with how the COVID-19 pandemic had been handled in this district despite the many challenges. A few students discussed how restorative practices helped them build positive relationships with their teachers and classmates. Some students testified that they could complete high school because of their school community support and the accountability measures established by restorative practices. While many came to publicly support Dr. Simmons, the board members received numerous complaints from teachers and administration in writing, along with no-confidence votes from the teachers' union and other prominent community members. They did not want to go on record but made it clear that they would remove their support for reelection if they voted to renew her contract. Three of the seven members were up for election and faced enormous pressure to vote against Dr. Simmons in spite of her positive performance and trajectory.

After the public testimony, the board members went into a closed session to discuss her fate. When they returned to face the public, the board president announced that it had been an extremely difficult deliberation. They acknowledged the progress made under Dr. Simmons's leadership but decided not to renew her contract for an additional three years. While Dr. Simmons was disappointed, she thanked the board for her time and exited the meeting. The room erupted in audible gasps and tears.

The next day, Dr. Simmons learned that students were planning a massive protest against the decision. Some of the seniors were willing to risk graduating on time if they participated. Deeply moved by their support but concerned about the potential harm to students, Dr. Simmons weighed her options. She considered how the board (her bosses) made the final decisions about the work she was able to do in the district. While they had been operating in the Dark Gray Phase by using their decisions to influence equitable change, they began to change with time to become lighter gray and performative in nature. In some cases, they were even willing to exhibit White Phase behavior by allowing the dialing back of much of the progress Dr. Simmons had led.

She knew that she would have options to serve students in another district because the search firm consistently reached out to her for other openings, primarily from districts that were ready for her type of leadership. Ultimately, she decided to accept the non-renewal and consider her next career steps. At the next school board meeting, she remarked:

> I am proud of what we've accomplished for the good of the district. I will always support this community. While I know many are planning to protest this decision, I humbly ask that we collectively support the non-renewal. For those in our community who support and appreciate the changes you have seen in the last four years, continue to advocate and press for what is right. To the board, when I was offered this opportunity to lead this district four years ago, your commitment was to the students, families, and communities. As the times changed, your commitment waned. I urge you to get back to what matters. The late, great Congresswoman Shirley Chisholm was the first Black woman to sit in the U.S. House of Representatives. Her campaign slogan in the 1972 Democratic presidential primary was "Unbought and unbossed." I urge you to search your minds and hearts to do the right thing!

Her supporters gave her a standing ovation, and Dr. Simmons left, knowing she had made the right, though painful, choice. She had planted the seeds of change and trusted they would continue to grow in her absence.

ANALYSIS

Some may view Dr. Simmons's story as tragic. But all too often, her story is a realistic outcome. Sometimes doing the right thing does not advance the leader, but it does advance the cause. She stood on her commitment to improving student instruction and well-being by establishing expectations and pathways to get qualified educators into the district; she was also subject to the human condition of her supervisors' unstable commitment that was beholden to special interests, which ultimately resulted in her nonrenewal.

When COVID-19 swept through the community, Dr. Simmons seized the opportunity to draw attention to the change that many aspired for marginalized students (Aspiration to Action). She mobilized district resources to address long-standing inequities. In a sense, she used the pandemic and the murder of George Floyd as levers to spark change (Symbols and Movements). During that time, she used the mandates and financial resources to equitably meet the needs of students, teachers, and schools (Comprehensive Codification). Dr. Simmons embraced the journey of doing what was right.

Even though her due diligence did not turn out as she would have liked, she held on to her integrity and values to advocate for and serve others. Dr. Martin Luther King, Jr. said, "The time is always right to do what is right." Even though some parts of Dr. Simmons's ICE-T attracted undeserved scrutiny and resistance, she used her spheres of influence and control to pursue equity. Her journey and accomplishments along the way are inherently just as important as the outcome.

Questions to Consider

1. What is the ultimate vision or long-term goal you hope to achieve through your equity advocacy, and how does this aspiration guide your actions and decisions in advancing equitable outcomes?
2. What movements or initiatives in your work or personal life have driven change toward greater equity or progress? Reflect on how these movements have been successful or where they have faced challenges, and consider what factors contributed to their outcomes.
3. What key comprehensive policies, procedures, or modifications provide the foundation for equity within your work context? How do they shape or influence equitable outcomes in your organization or field?

CHAPTER 7

So What? Now, What?

Applying the Equity Empowerment Continuum in Your Work

When facilitating professional development workshops, I typically end with, "So what? Now, What?" The EEC is a way to think about how and to what degree you will act to achieve an equitable end. Having spent time in both the academy and practice, I understand that practitioners need some concrete steps to take. In this final chapter, I will provide some reflective tools to take on your journey to ensure that you can choose actions that can result in progress.

In this book, I have discussed the importance of timing, or the "T" in your ICE-T. Sometimes change is embraced to meet the needs of less served individuals or groups. At other times, there is heightened resistance change. However, Dr. King said, "The time is always right to do what is right." There will always be a reason to advocate for yourself and others. There is never a final equity pinnacle because times and contexts will always change, which provides opportunities for new equity considerations. The EEC is a tool that considers the ever-changing context and timing of issues related to power and resources. This book addresses the landscape that continues to evolve with respect to equity. The dynamic environment cannot stop the work that must be done to provide more equitable outcomes. Your ICE-T (Identity, Context, Experiences, and Timing) is the foundation of your decision-making.

Once you consider what phase you may be in or what identifiers you may experience, you are able to begin to consider how you will push through the shades of gray. You must get specific about your goals, the challenges you face, and what assets and attributes you have to work through them so you can begin to push through the shades of gray. This final chapter will provide an ongoing check-in process and suggestions for you to move forward through the shades of gray. The chapter closes with some suggestions to help you "weather the storms" and the challenges of pushing through the shades of gray.

GETTING CLEAR (GETTING ON THE SAME PAGE)

EQUITY GOALS

In many cases, the charge to implement an equity agenda comes with little direction on how to achieve equity. In some cases, due to intentional confusion, people do not really understand exactly what the basic definition of equity is or what an equity codification should accomplish. There is no one way to best approach your task. Throughout this book, one specific equity program or system has not been promoted for adoption. The EEC is a supplemental conceptual mapping to help you monitor and manage your progress.

Chapter 1 discusses the proliferation of programs and books that promote equity work. Each field has various suggested initiatives that promise to create more equitable outcomes for those in the organization and those served by the organization. To be effective, you should research the prominent equity strategies and approaches and choose the programs and strategies that most align with the mission and direction your organization is taking with regard to addressing equity issues.

Most effective programs include self-awareness, examining current practices and policies, and creating a strategic plan to address equity challenges within the organization. An equity win would be to see the efforts written in policy and standard operating procedures. Within strategic planning, specific goals should be set with accountability.

During my time as an equity leader, I drew from the work of the Pacific Education Group's professional development program, Beyond Diversity, and *Courageous Conversations about Race* (Singleton, 2021), the book that underpinned it. I was fortunate enough to have individuals from our state instruction department fund my attendance at training along with board members and other key stakeholders. This training allowed us to develop a common language to discuss equity challenges or lack of cultural responsiveness.

Another framework that informed my work was the Wisconsin Response to Intervention (RtI) Center's Model to Inform Culturally Responsive Practice (2017). The framework is extremely helpful in enabling district and school staff understand a clinical process to becoming a more equitable individual and organization as a whole. This model was informed by the work of Drs. Gloria Ladson-Billing, a K-12 influential scholar, along with Drs. Anthony Muhammad and Sharokie Hollie, two prolific practitioner-scholars who have informed school leadership and practical pedagogy. While this model is intended for understanding and combating equitable actions within education, it can apply to any field. I have worked with organizations outside of education and modified the model to address other professions and fields.

REFLECTION

What equity frameworks, books, or programs do you personally or professionally rely on to guide your equity work? Does everyone in your professional setting understand how these equity resources inform and guide the overall equity goals?

The EEC Goals Assessment encourages analyzes your goals based on the elements of the EEC. Form 7.1 connects your equity goal (s) to the EEC.

EQUITY GOAL(S)

- Write the specific equity-related goal(s) and why they are important.
- Describe how these goals are aligned with your values.
- Describe how the selected phases/Identifiers relate to where you are on the equity continuum.
- Determine your ICE-T.
    - What part of your ICE-T can help move your equity goal forward?
    - In your network, whose ICE-T can be helpful in moving your equity goal forward?
- Assess your spheres of influence and control.
    - Identify spheres of control.
    - Identify spheres of influence.
    - Identify what is outside of your control and how to navigate those things.

Once your organization has determined the system and strategies, common languages and ways to understand progress must be developed. Use the language and frameworks adopted by the organization to facilitate professional learning. In most trainings, I would use the language by making visual connections between the frameworks and approaches so that the staff could see how the equity training related to their daily work. Using a common language and connecting equity professional learning to the work already done will help people integrate equity within all facets of the organization.

FORM 7.1 ● The EEC Goal Assessment

Write the specific equity-related goal(s) and why they are important.	

Check areas where you may be on the continuum.

WHITE	LIGHT GRAY	DARK GRAY	BLACK
• Avoidance • Misinformation • Dialing back progress	• Performance Allyship • Kicking can down the road • No money where your mouth is	• Maximizing your networks • Using your ICE-T to create Win-Wins • Written Accountability	• Aspiration • Movements • Comprehensive Codification

Describe how the selected phases/Identifiers relate to where you are on the equity continuum.

___

___

___

___

Iced tea photo by iStock.com/chas53

What part of your ICE-T can help move your equity goal forward?

In your network, whose ICE-T can be helpful in moving your equity goal forward?

Identify spheres of control

Identify spheres of influence

Identify what is outside of your control and how to navigate those things

EQUITY EMPOWERMENT CONTINUUM ASSESSMENT

Reflection is a critical skill all formal and informal leaders must possess. As mentioned in chapter 4, many schools or districts follow a continuous improvement cycle to monitor progress on important academic or programmatic goals. This cycle includes a process called Plan (P), Do (D), Check (C), and Act (A) (Continuous Improvement, 2024). Many other fields outside educational also use the PDCA implementation strategy as well. The cycle implies that the process is ongoing, which calls for you and/or a team to consistently be reflective of the progress made as you work toward implementing your equity goals. Continuous improvement implies that something can always be improved. As either a formal or informal equity leader, you must consistently keep a reflection mindset (Aguilar, 2016). As you assess the progress and impact made by your work efforts, additional resources and strategies may be needed to achieve the goal (Continuous Improvement, 2024). This process will cause you to be flexible within your context and within the inevitable resistance you will face. Equity leaders must consistently reflect on their values, beliefs, and personal histories (within this book, also known as ICE-T) to maximize leadership and advancement of equity goals (Aguilar, 2016).

The EEC Equity Goal Check-in can assist you with reflecting upon the progress made toward the equity goal(s). After establishing your goals and determining how your ICE-T and spheres of influence can impact your work (Form 7.2), it is critical that you build upon the work that has been done. Starting from scratch can place your work within the white or light gray phases by avoiding the work needed or "kicking the can down the road" for inconsistent results. Monitoring the work by understanding what has been learned from previous and current successes and failures can determine how the equity goal(s) is met in the future. Once you have decided, this tool asks you to identify what impact you are actually having on the organization. It is important to assess the impact your efforts have had on the issues of inequity or injustice. Form 7.2 is a personal EEC check-in and Form 7.3 can be used to assess a team's progress on equity goals.

FORM 7.2 ● The Equity Empowerment Continuum Personal Check-In

These questions should be asked at the beginning of your equity-related personal work. As part of a continuous improvement cycle, select a check-in time and ask these questions to monitor growth and make adjustments.

EQUITY GOAL(S)	
Write the specific equity-related goal(s) and why they are important.	
Describe how these goals are aligned with your values.	

PROGRESS	
Identify the progress made toward the equity goal(s).	
Describe what you have done that has been most effective to this point.	

LESSONS & GROWTH	
Describe the challenges you have experienced working toward your equity goal (s).	
List in bullets the lessons learned as a result of your equity efforts.	

(Continued)

(Continued)

IMPACT & CONTRIBUTIONS	
Describe the impact your work has had on your community or organization.	

SPHERE OF INFLUENCE & CONTROL	
List who are within my sphere of control.	
List who I can influence related to my equity goals.	
Describe what is outside my sphere of influence and what I must do to address and navigate those things.	

NEXT STEPS	
Idenify what We need to know about moving our equity goal(s) forward.	
What can We do to "push through" the identifier?	
How can our collective ICE-T move us forward?	

FORM 7.3 ● The Equity Empowerment Continuum Group/Organization Check-In

These questions should be asked at the beginning of your equity-related group/organization's work. As part of a continuous improvement cycle, select a check-in time and ask these questions to monitor growth and make adjustments.

EQUITY GOAL(S)	
Write our specific equity-related goal(s) and why they are important to us.	
Describe how these goals are aligned with our values.	

PROGRESS	
Identify the progress made toward our equity goal(s).	
Describe what we have done that has been has been most effective to this point.	

LESSONS & GROWTH	
Describe the challenges we have experienced working toward our equity goal (s).	
List in bullets the lessons we learned due to our equity efforts.	

(Continued)

(Continued)

IMPACT & CONTRIBUTIONS	
Describe the impact our work has had on our community or organization.	

SPHERE OF INFLUENCE & CONTROL	
List who are within our sphere of control.	
List who we can influence related to our equity goals.	
Describe what is outside our sphere of influence and control and what we must do to address and navigate those things.	

NEXT STEPS	
Identify what we need to know about moving our equity goal(s) forward.	
What can we do to "push through" the identifier?	
How can our collective ICE-T move us forward?	

PROGRESS

- Identify the progress made toward the equity goal(s).
- Describe what you have done that has been most effective to this point.

LESSONS & GROWTH

- Describe the challenges you have experienced working toward your equity goal (s).
- List in bullets the lessons learned as a result of your equity efforts.

IMPACT & CONTRIBUTIONS

- Describe the impact your work has had on your community or organization.

SPHERE OF INFLUENCE & CONTROL

- List those within my sphere of control.
- List those I can influence related to my equity goals.
- Describe what is outside my sphere of influence and what I must do to address and navigate those things.

NEXT STEPS

- Identify what I need to know about moving my equity goal(s) forward.
- What can I do to "push through" the identifier?
- How can my ICE-T move me forward?

WELLNESS CHECKS

Geronimus (2023) says that people who focus on issues of advocating for equitable outcomes can be impacted by "weathering." This is the physical wear and tear on people who are fighting against injustices. She shares that Dr. Martin Luther King's autopsy revealed that although he was murdered at thirty-nine, his heart was reflective of a sixty-year-old man. Of course, there are several possible reasons why someone's heart can be compromised and damaged at a young age, including genetic predisposition, lack of exercise and rest, and poor eating habits. However, Geronimus speculates that his heart's condition was due to "the fact that he lived continuously on alert to threats, maintaining his composure, nonetheless, and in survival mode." This chronic vigilance and adaptation take a huge health toll on the human biological canvas—a condition known as "weathering."

Like "weathering," William A. Smith (2014) coined the term *racial battle fatigue* initially to address how Black men experienced predominately white colleges and universities. In his research, he describes the physical, emotional, and psychological burden placed on Black men as they encounter racial discrimination and profiling. This idea was built upon the concept of combat stress syndrome, which describes how people who live and work in hostile environments navigate those environments. *Racial battle fatigue* presents several symptoms, including stress, agitation, worry, and other physical conditions. Inevitably, racial battle fatigue impacts Black men's academic and professional lives (Smith et al., 2016, Smith et al., 2020).

Both terms, *weathering* and *racial battle fatigue*, can be applied to the experience that activists or advocates for marginalized identities outside of race encounter. Theoharis (2007) studied school principals with social justice or equity dispositions. One important finding from his study is that the principals reacted differently to the resistance to their efforts. Some experienced physical, emotional, and mental stress, which manifested in nausea, unexplained crying, and lack of sleep. Others experienced depression and other health-related conditions from consistent exposure to pressure and lack of self-care. As a result of this pressure, some of the principals developed bad habits that were harmful mentally and physically, like becoming workaholics and abusing alcohol.

REFLECTION

Describe a time when you were mentally and/or physically tired and exhausted from advocating for equitable change in your personal or professional setting.

Chen and Gorski (2015) find that those who focus on social justice or human rights issues are more likely to experience burnout. Their study of twenty-two social justice and human rights activists found that a "culture of martyrdom" is prevalent amongst activists and advocates for social justice. Scott (2019) describes a "culture of martyrdom" where sacrificing oneself and wellness for the greater good is admired. In other words, even though the activist described their burnout as a result of the challenging work, it was expected and celebrated among colleagues.

As a college sophomore, I was the recording secretary for the Black Student Council. As on many predominantly white campuses (PWIs) nationwide, over the years, there have always been some challenges with how students of color interact on the campus. During my term, we decided to address the issue of why students of color were not consistently picked up by the campus transportation unless they had backpacks on and were clearly identified as students. The campus is located downtown, where the city's citizens frequently intermingle with students. The transportation pick-up protocol was that students could catch the campus transportation either at a station or they could wave one of the vehicles down anywhere on campus, and the van was to pull over and pick the student up. Unfortunately, I, along with other Black students, had been regularly passed up if we were not at a designated stop.

As a result, we started a campaign to draw attention to this disparity. Amid everything, we contacted the NAACP and held a televised press conference. I remember being so livid because I felt unheard and, literally, unseen. The university seemed slow to respond and disingenuous about providing a tangible resolution to our concerns. It enraged me. I started feeling physically sick. My typical terse, sharp responses were even more intense. After weeks of this, our president said to me, "Latish, you don't want to end up losing your mind over this. You may end up hurting yourself or somebody else." My passion had bubbled over into something that was visibly dangerous to my peers. It took me by surprise because I had not understood the impact this situation was having on my mental and physical health.

In the EEC's Black Phase, aspiration to action is an important identifier that represents the collective passion needed to pursue justice or more equitable outcomes. Your efforts may not pan out if you have no aspirations and are not passionate about your work. However, fighting injustice is filled with passion that can consume you. If you are not well, the change you endeavor to create could be cut short by illness, a broken personal life, or worse yet, death. Many equity leaders, past and present, likely experienced weathering to some degree and accepted the culture of martyrdom, which enabled them to pursue the work or be consumed by the work, in some ways no longer effective in the work or worse yet, dead.

CHECKING-IN & COPING

> "Caring for myself is not self-indulgence, it is self-preservation, and that is an act of political warfare."
>
> —Audre Lourde

During the pandemic, we learned that masks could be a tool in keeping us safe from spreading viruses to others. Even before the pandemic, if you have ever flown on an airplane, the airline attendants always instruct people to secure their masks before anyone else's if the cabin pressure drops and oxygen is needed. You are encouraged to put your mask on even before assisting small children. In both instances, the message is to take care of yourself before you help others. Similarly, to execute and sustain your equity goals, you must ensure that you consistently check your wellness.

It is crucial for those engaged in advocacy to make sure that they take care of themselves by engaging in holistic physical, emotional, and spiritual activities (Pitts, 2023). If needed, therapy or other intentional cultural healing practices can address gaps in the wellness of social justice advocates. Also, it is helpful to establish and keep regular routines that address self-care, and boundaries, and reach out to those in your community for support when needed.

The principals in Theoharis's (2007) study used several ways to cope with the challenges related to resistance in their equity work. They preemptively developed coping strategies to navigate the challenges of their jobs as social justice school leaders. These strategies included using purposeful communication, creating and using supportive networks, including staff in decision-making, prioritizing tasks, providing professional learning, and keeping relationships at the core. Due to these practices, the leaders reported feeling less isolated and stressed out during their challenging journey. To maintain wellness, the principals instituted practices such as creating boundaries between work and personal life, taking up hobbies outside of work, staying physically active, and volunteering.

It is possible to pursue equitable outcomes without causing irreversible harm to yourself. It is also a part of the long-term political strategy to sustain equity work (Hernández Cárdenas & Tello Méndez, 2017). You must honor yourself with proper self-care so as not to undermine your important equity goals (Pitts, 2023). Even though there may be a culture of glorifying hard work that can cause personal demise, it is critical that we prioritize self-care. If you do not, it will deepen the inequities for the communities needing support and advocacy.

REFLECTION

What self-care regimens keep you healthy, mentally and physically?

The second tool is a wellness-check assessment to determine how you are doing due to the equity work you are engaged in. When I was a middle school teacher, one of my veteran colleagues suggested a technique to quickly provide students with feedback on their work or performance. The strategy calls for the "glows" and "grows." The glows represent what was done well in the assignment or performance tasks. On the other hand, the "grows" identify where the student can improve.

REFLECTION

In the face of everyday challenges such as burnout, emotional labor, and fatigue, how can you establish and maintain boundaries that protect your mental and physical well-being while continuing to push forward in your equity work?

Forms 7.4 and 7.5 are individual and group Wellness Checks, respectively. As an educator who has transitioned into a leadership coach, I have implemented this same strategy while working with clients. The Wellness Check-in tool asks you and/or your team to identify the following glows:

- What is going well in this work?
- What is my "happy place" in this work?
- What am I grateful for outside of this work? And how does it replenish me?

The following questions help you or your team identify grows or areas that may need attention to sustain the work you are doing:

- What is not going well in this work?
- WINN – What do I need *now?*
- How am I dealing with the things that are not going well?
- How do the challenges make me feel physically? Mentally? Spiritually?
- What part of the challenges are outside of my control? Considering these things, what can I release?
- Considering my identified challenges, who can I include as a trusted thought partner?

FORM 7.4 • The Equity Empowerment Continuum Individual Wellness Check-In

These questions should be asked periodically to ensure you are "weathering the storms" and the challenges associated with pushing through the shades of gray. Be well!

WELLNESS GLOWS	
What is going well in this work?	
What is my "happy place" in this work?	
What am I grateful for outside of this work? And how does it replenish me?	

WELLNESS GROWS	
What is not going well in this work?	
WINN - What do I need *now*?	
How am I dealing with the things that are not going well?	
How do the challenges make me feel physically? Mentally? Spiritually?	
What part of the challenges are outside of my control? Considering these things, what can I release?	
Considering my challenges, who can I include as a trusted thought partner?	

FORM 7.5 • The Equity Empowerment Continuum Group Wellness Check-In

These questions should be asked periodically to ensure that your group or organization is "weathering the storms" and addressing the challenges associated with pushing through the shades of gray. Take an inventory of everyone's responses. Find common things to determine collective wellness. Pay attention to outlying responses to support members struggling more than the rest of the group. In addition, identify those who are strong and consider ways to support their lift. Be well!

WELLNESS GLOWS	
What is going well in this work?	
What is our "happy place" in this work?	
What are we grateful for outside of this work? And how does it replenish us?	

WELLNESS GROWS	
What is not going well in this work?	
WINN - What do we need *now*?	
How are we dealing with the things that are not going well?	
How do the challenges make us feel physically? Mentally? Spiritually?	
What part of the challenges are outside of our control? Considering these things, what can we release?	
Considering our challenges, how do we discuss and positively problem-solve them?	

FINAL VIGNETTE

In the final vignette, I share an assessment of my own equity work based on the EEC, goal check-in, and wellness check. The elements discussed in this chapter are used to evaluate personal and organizational influence. First, I will discuss my work based on the EEC goals framework. Overall, I would classify the work I facilitated as a named equity leader as being between the light gray and dark gray phases. The district administrators and board of directors at that time seemed to have a clear commitment to increasing equity within the organization. As the equity focus was a new initiative, it was not clear what resources were needed to fully carry out the vision and mission of increased equity goals. Even with that said, the goal was to create an equity policy to drive the work in the mission. I maximized my sphere of influence by making sure that all the things I was tasked with were planned and executed well. While the resources were few and the actual budget under my purview was small, I built relationships across the organization, which helped influence those with decision-making power.

In many instances, my ICE-T worked in my favor. But, in other cases, it worked against me. As a woman of color advocating on behalf of a district filled with students of color, I was able to passionately use my voice to lift the need for more equitable practices. At the same time, I knew that because of that shared identity, many refused to listen. For that reason, I learned to use my sphere of influence and my networks to lift the same messages about the need for policy, programmatic, and resource changes. I identified factors outside my control and communicated with others about the best strategies to navigate these challenges. The codification of an equity policy and revisions to the gender identity and nondiscrimination policy marked significant advancements. However, I often felt frustrated that some efforts seemed performative; we made strong statements but lacked the resources or strategy to implement them. Additionally, many issues were postponed because people were hesitant to enact some of the best practices. I encountered many self-proclaimed allies who avoided addressing issues due to fear of backlash. This work often felt like dancing the cha-cha—progressing on some days and encountering resistance on others.

Despite these challenges, many things were working well. I had the opportunity to collaborate with several leaders and departments to initiate equity and culturally responsive practices within their areas. I built rapport with numerous stakeholders across the district and supported various organizational decisions. An equity policy was passed with directives to create guidance for equity across the entire district. However, my influence waned with the shift in leadership. I had even less autonomy to utilize the funding set aside for equity work.

The new administration did not value my input as much, reducing the planned progress. I decided to shift my energy to maintain my well-being and continue my work. An opportunity to join the professional development team became available, and I ultimately became a professional development manager. This role allowed me to work with various departments across the organization. Leveraging the rapport and influence I had built through my work in equity and culturally responsive practices, I supported colleagues in creating professional learning opportunities for teachers, staff, and leaders in the district. Although my role was no longer as a named equity leader, I continued to lead professional development with an equity lens.

As mentioned earlier in this book, I live with Lupus, a debilitating disease characterized by flare-ups often triggered by stress. Over three years, I experienced several flare-ups, most of which were mild, but one resulted in hospitalization and three weeks away from work. Mentally, I disliked the person I was becoming—angry and defensive, similar to how I felt as an undergraduate. I understood that most resistance was not personal but stemmed from people's reluctance to change practices or reallocate resources equitably. However, I began to take the opposition personally, feeling defeated and depressed, eventually needing medical attention.

At that time, being an equity leader had become overwhelming. Once, my sister visited me for a week while I was in the role. She watched as I juggled work, ranted about job stressors, woke up early to address important emails, and got my son off to school. She concluded that the pace was unsustainable. Many single moms navigate their professions successfully, but she focused on the specific stress of feeling unsafe at work, which ultimately threatened my physical and mental health.

Despite the challenges, I found joy in certain aspects of the job. I met incredible people who went above and beyond their job descriptions to support the work. Colleagues from different departments eagerly volunteered to serve on committees and facilitate professional learning sessions. Seeing so many people committed to equity work was encouraging. Additionally, I was deeply grateful for my son. When I began the role, he was a young child, and I had previously been in academia, allowing me more flexibility to be present in his life. I enjoyed picking him up from school and being there for important moments. However, with my new job, he often had to spend time in before- and aftercare. Nonetheless, he remained an inspiration to me, and I cherished my role as his mother.

Unfortunately, many aspects of the job were not going well. I needed consistent and strong leadership to continue the work I was hired to do, but I struggled with the lack of it. Physically, I began to fall ill. The stress from work affected my family life and personal well-being. I became extremely discouraged and despondent. The challenges outweighed the benefits and impact I could make. While I had a support system of colleagues, after discussing my situation with them, they helped me realize I needed to prioritize my health. As a single mother caring for my son, it was crucial for me to be well for him.

Recognizing the need to prioritize my health, I reassessed my wellness. After considering the decline in my mental and physical health, I decided to take a lateral position without an equity focus. In retrospect, leaving my equity role and taking intentional time to care for my wellness made me realize that I could have sustained myself better if I had prioritized my self-care.

My real-life memoir experience of being an equity leader and being a part of many others who desired to lead in equitable ways demonstrates the complexity of equity work. The most transformative lesson I want you to take away is that no matter how the context and timing change, you can always be flexible enough to continue the work with renewed purpose and balance. I often think about the many heroes I hold in high esteem who have accomplished great strides toward equality, equity, and justice. Many factors affected their ultimate impact on the work. What is certain is that they had to choose when crucial changes in their work and their personal lives came up. In my case, making a change in the work allowed me to collaborate with more colleagues and embed equity and cultural responsiveness within the context of professional development, albeit in a new context. Embracing this change improved my well-being and reaffirmed my commitment to the cause, proving that there are multiple pathways to making a significant impact.

Questions to Consider

1. How often do you engage in personal reflection about your equity work? What have been your recent "glows" (successes) and "grows" (areas for improvement) as a leader or advocate for equity?
2. Reflect on how you incorporate wellness checks into your work. What strategies do you use to prevent burnout, and how can you build more intentional self-care practices into your routine?
3. Think about a time when you faced significant resistance to equity work. How did you cope with the stress and pressure? In retrospect, what could you have done differently to manage your well-being while maintaining progress?

References

PREFACE

Barrow, B. (2024). *Donald Trump has sweeping plans for a second administration. Here's what he's proposed.* Associated Press. https://apnews.com/article/donald-trump-wins-second-term-policies-de3dcf0f173b42602b258042fd7aaafb

Bennett, B., Berenson Rogers, T. (2020). How Donald Trump lost the election. *Time.* https://time.com/5907973/donald-trump-loses-2020-election/

Dimock, M. (2017). *How America changed during Barack Obama's presidency.* The Pew Institute. https://www.pewresearch.org/social-trends/2017/01/10/how-america-changed-during-barack-obamas-presidency/

Fram, A., Lemire, J. (2018). *Trump: Why allow immigrants from 'shithole countries'?* Associated Press. https://apnews.com/article/immigration-north-america-donald-trump-ap-top-news-international-news-fdda2ff0b877416c8ae1c1a77a3cc425

Kors. S. (2012). Book Review: The Obama question: A progressive perspective. *Columbia Magazine Online.* https://magazine.columbia.edu/article/book-review-obama-question-progressive-perspective

Lilly Ledbetter Fair Pay Act of 2009, Pub. L. No. 111-2, 123 Stat. 5 (2009). https://www.congress.gov/111/plaws/publ2/PLAW-111publ2.pdf

Rascoe, A. (2021). *For 1st time in 150 years, outgoing president doesn't attend inauguration.* National Public Radio. https://www.npr.org/2021/01/20/958905703/for-1st-time-in-150-years-outgoing-president-doesnt-attend-inauguration

Schorr, D. (2008). *A new, 'post-racial' political era in America.* National Public Radio. https://www.npr.org/2008/01/28/18489466/a-new-post-racial-political-era-in-america

Trump, D. J. (2015, June 16). *Donald Trump Presidential Announcement Speech.* P2016, Race for the White House, Press Releases, Advisories, Statements. https://www.p2016.org/trump/trump061615sp.html

U.S. Department of Health and Human Services. (n.d.). *About the ACA.* https://www.hhs.gov/healthcare/about-the-aca/index.html

Willer, R., Feinberg, M., & Wetts, R. (2016). *Threats to racial status promote Tea Party support among white Americans.* SSRN. https://papers.ssrn.com/sol3/papers.cfm?abstract_id=2770186

INTRODUCTION

Anders, G. (2023). *Who's vaulting into the C-suite? Trends changed fast in 2022.* LinkedIn. https://www.linkedin.com/pulse/whos-vaulting-c-suite-trends-changed-fast-2022-george-anders/

Denaby, D. (1989). He's gotta have it. *New York Magazine/Vulture.* https://www.vulture.com/article/movie-review-spike-lee-do-the-right- thing.html

Diangelo, R. (2018). *White fragility: Why it's so hard for white people to talk about racism.* Beacon Press.

Feldblum, C., & Lipnic, V. A. (2016). *Select task force on the study of harassment in the workplace.* U.S. Equal Employment Opportunity Commission. https://www.eeoc.gov/select-task-force-study-harassmentworkplace#_Toc453686298

Fernandes, N. (2021). Belonging: The intersection of DEI and engagement. *Forbes.* https://www.forbes.com/sites/forbeshumanresourcescouncil/2021/12/22/belonging-the-intersection-of-dei-and-engagement

Hopke, T. (2022). White men are feeling left out of diversity, equity, & inclusion. Why should we care and what should we do? *Forbes*. https://www.forbes.com/sites/teresahopke/2022/03/30/white-men-are-feeling-left-out-of-dei-diversity-equity--inclusion-why-should-we-care-and-what-should-we-do/?sh=3dc5d39cfaa6

Hsu, A. (2023). Corporate DEI initiatives are facing cutbacks and legal attacks. *NPR*. https://www.npr.org/2023/08/19/1194595310/dei-affirmative-action-supreme-court-layoffs-diversity-equity-inclusion

Kendi, I. X. (2023). *How to be an antiracist*. One World.

Lee, S. (n.d.). Critics said do the right thing would 'incite riots. *The Guardian*. https://www.theguardian.com/film/2023/sep/11/spike-lee-critics-said-do-the-right-thing-would-incite-riots

LinkedIn. (n.d.). *The rise of diversity and inclusion roles across Europe and the Middle East*. https://business.linkedin.com/talent-solutions/resources/talent-acquisition/the-rise-of-diversity-and-inclusion

Mattice, C. (2023). *What diversity, equity and inclusion really mean*. LinkedIn. https://www.linkedin.com/pulse/what-diversity-equity-inclusion-really-mean-catherine/

Maurer, R. (2020). New DE&I roles spike after racial justice protests. *SHRM*. https://www.shrm.org/topics-tools/news/talent-acquisition/new-dei-roles-spike-racial-justice-protests

Murray, J. K. (2023). *Jobs in diversity, inclusion and belonging have risen 123% since May—here's how to get one*. Indeed. https://www.indeed.com/career-advice/finding-a-job/diversity-inclusion-and-belonging-jobs-rise

Pulver, A. (2023) Spike Lee: Critics said *Do the Right Thing* would 'incite riots.' *The Guardian*. https://www.theguardian.com/film/2023/sep/11/spike-lee-critics-said-do-the-right-thing-would-incite-riots

Salter, J. (2021). 2 views of Floyd onlookers: Desperate to help, or angry mob. *Associated Press*. https://apnews.com/article/closing-arguments-chauvin-trial-bystanders-dadc00a65723b4ea2c507aff4471d364

Singleton, G. (2021). *Courageous conversations about race: A field guide for achieving equity in schools and beyond* (3rd ed.). Corwin.

Siskel and Ebert Movie Reviews (1989). *10 Best Films of the 1980s*. https://siskelebert.org/?p=480

Zheng, L. (2020). Do your employees feel safe reporting abuse and discrimination? *Harvard Business Review*. https://hbr.org/2020/10/do-your-employees-feel-safe-reporting-abuse-and-discrimination

CHAPTER 1

Anti-Defamation League. (2014). *The N-Word: Its history, use, and impact*. https://www.adl.org/resources/lesson-plan/n-word-its-history-use-and-impact

Chang, H. (2016). *Autoethnography as method*. Routledge.

Dillard, C. B. (2000). The substance of things hoped for, the evidence of things not seen: Examining an endarkened feminist epistemology in educational research and leadership. *International Journal of Qualitative Studies in Education*, *13*(6), 661-681.

Douglass, F. (2018). *Narrative of the life of Frederick Douglass, an American slave*. Broadview Press.

Eligon, M. (2020, June). A debate over identity and race asks, are African-Americans 'Black' or 'black'? *New York Times*. https://www.nytimes.com/2020/06/26/us/black-african-american-style-debate.html

Haley, A., & Shabazz, A. (1989). *The autobiography of Malcolm X*. Ballantine Books.

Hollie, S. (2017). *Culturally and linguistically responsive teaching and learning: Classroom practices for student success*. Teacher Created Materials.

Lindsey, G. (2024, June 14). *Why do people say AKS instead of ASK?* [Video]. YouTube. https://www.youtube.com/watch?v=3nysHgnXx-o

MacNeill, A. (2019, June 4). 'We cannot squander this moment': 5 key quotes from Anita Hill's graduation speech at Wellesley College. *Boston.com*. https://www.boston.com/

news/local-news/2019/06/04/anita-hill-wellesley-college-graduation-speech/

Malesky, K. (2014, March). The journey from 'Colored' to 'Minorities' to 'People Of Color'. *NPR*. https://www.npr.org/sections/codeswitch/2014/03/30/295931070/the-journey-from-colored-to-minorities-to-people-of-color

Mock, F. (2013). *Anita: Speaking truth to power* [Film]. American Film Foundation, Chanlim Films, Impact Partners, Artemis Rising Foundation, and ITVS.

National Association for the Advancement of Colored People (NAACP). (2014). *NAACP official position on the use of the word "Nigger" and the "N" word*. https://naacp.org/resources/naacp-official-position-use-word-nigger-and-n-word

Random House. (2017, November 7). *Ta-Nehisi Coates on words that don't belong to everyone* [Video]. Youtube. https://www.youtube.com/watch?v=QO15S3WC9pg

Singleton, G. E. (2021). *Courageous conversations about race: A field guide for achieving equity in schools*. Corwin Press.

Snyder, M. M. (2015). Leaning into autoethnography: a review of Heewon Chang's autoethnography as method. *The Qualitative Report, 20*(2), 93-96.

Wilkinson, B. (2021). Diversity gap: Where good intentions meet true cultural change. Harper-Collins Leadership.

Wisconsin Department of Public Instruction. (2017). *Equity: Wisconsin's model to inform culturally responsive practices*. https://dpi.wi.gov/emlss/equity

CHAPTER 2

Giebelhaus, J., Greenfield-Sanders, T., Thompson, C., Walker, T., (Producers) & Greenfield-Sanders, T. (Director). (2019). *Toni Morrison: The Pieces I Am*. [Film]

Haworth, J. (2021, February). Aunt Jemima announces new name, removes 'racial stereotypes' from product. *ABC News*. https://abcnews.go.com/US/aunt-jemima-announces-removes-racial-stereotypes-product/story?id=75797458

Li, S. (2009). *Toni Morrison: A biography*. Greenwood Publishing Group.

Rose, C. (2015, September 4). *Toni Morrison beautifully answers an 'Illegitimate' question on race (Jan. 19, 1998)*. https://www.youtube.com/watch?v=-Kgq3F8wbYA

Vanzant, I. (Executive Producer). (2012–2021). *Fix my life* [TV series]. Pigeon, Inc.; Oprah Winfrey Network.

Wendt, J. (2017, February 12). *Toni Morrison interview*. YouTube. https://www.youtube.com/watch?v=DQ0mMjII22I

CHAPTER 3

Anderson, J. (Host). (2013–Present). The state of critical race theory in education [Audio podcast]. *The Harvard Edcast*. https://www.gse.harvard.edu/ideas/edcast/22/02/state-critical-race-theory-education

Berg, J. A., & Woods, N. F. (2023). Overturning *Roe v. Wade*: Consequences for midlife women's health and well-being. *Womens Midlife Health*, 9(2). https://womensmidlifehealthjournal.biomedcentral.com/articles/10.1186/s40695-022-00085-8

Bose, N. (2022). *Roe v Wade ruling disproportionately hurts Black women, experts say*. https://www.reuters.com/world/us/roe-v-wade-ruling-disproportionately-hurts-black-women-experts-say-2022-06-27/

Britannica (2024). White. In *Britannica*. https://www.britannica.com/search?query=white

Brown v. Board of Education, 347 U.S. 483 (1954)

Center for Disease Control. (1991). *Current trends mortality attributable to HIV infection/AIDS -- United States, 1981-1990*. https://www.cdc.gov/mmwr/preview/mmwrhtml/00001880.htm

Creary, S. (2024). *Is DEI going away? here's what experts say*. Knowledge at Wharton. https://knowledge.wharton.upenn.edu/article/is-dei-going-away-heres-what-experts-say/

Davies, D. (2023, March 21). *Private opulence, public squalor: How the U.S. helps the rich and hurts the poor*.

https://www.npr.org/sections/health-shots/2023/03/21/1164275807/poverty-by-america-matthew-desmond-inequality

DiAngelo, R. (2018). *White fragility: Why it's so hard for white people to talk about racism*. Beacon Press.

Fisher v. University of Texas at Austin, 579 US _ (2016). https://www.oyez.org/cases/2015/14-981

George, J. (2020). A lesson on critical race theory. *Human Rights, 46*, 2.

GLAAD (2024). Moms for Liberty (M4L). https://glaad.org/gap/moms-liberty/

Hannah-Jones, N., & Watson, R. (2021). *The 1619 project: Born on the water*. Penguin.

Hassanein, N. (2022). People of color, the poor and other marginalized people to bear the brunt if Roe v. Wade is overturned. *USA TODAY*. https://www.usatoday.com/story/news/health/2022/05/03/people-color-most-impacted-if-roe-v-wade-overturned/9626866002/

Health Resources & Services Administration. (n.d.). *Who was Ryan White?* https://ryanwhite.hrsa.gov/about/ryan-white

Horowitz, J. M., Igielnik, R., & Kochhar, R. (2020). *Most Americans say there is too much economic inequality in the US, but fewer than half call it a top priority*. Pew Research. https://www.pewresearch.org/social-trends/2020/01/09/most-americans-say-there-is-too-much-economic-inequality-in-the-u-s-but-fewer-than-half-call-it-a-top-priority/

Johnson, A. M. (2015, December 30). *Defining implicit bias and racial anxiety*. YouTube. https://www.youtube.com/watch?v=msscegmQpW0&t=1s

Ladson-Billings, G. (1995). But that's just good teaching! The case for culturally relevant pedagogy. *Theory Into Practice, 34*(3), 159–165.

Ladson-Billings, G. (2014). Culturally relevant pedagogy 2.0: a.k.a. the remix. *Harvard Educational Review, 84*(1), 74–84.

Maddox, C. (2022, January 12). Literacy by any means necessary: The history of anti-literacy laws in the U.S. *Oakland Literacy Coalition*. https://oaklandliteracycoalition.org/literacy-by-any-means-necessary-the-history-of-anti-literacy-laws-in-the-u-s/

McCann, A., Schoenfeld Walker, A., Sasani, A., Johnston, T., Buchanan, L., Huang, J., Sanger-Katz, M., & Zernike, K. (2024). Tracking abortion bans across the country. *The New York Times*. https://www.nytimes.com/interactive/2022/us/abortion-laws-roe-v-wade.html

National Association of Independent Schools, (2015, December 30). *Defining Implicit Bias and Racial Anxiety* [video]. YouTube. https://youtube/msscegmQpW0?si=o1ukBkDgfcOZsCJp

Parker, E. T. III. (2023). *What's lost in dismantling DEI offices*. Inside Higher Ed. https://www.insidehighered.com/opinion/views/2024/02/19/whats-lost-dismantling-dei-offices-opinion

Reagan's Response. (n.d.). *Georgia state university library*. https://exhibits.library.gsu.edu/out-in-the-archives/hiv-aids/reagans-response/

Reilly, K. (2022). Florida's governor just signed the 'Stop Woke Act.' Here's what it means for schools and businesses. *Times Magazine*. https://time.com/6168753/florida-stop-woke-law/

Roe v. Wade, 410 U.S. 113 (1973). https://www.oyez.org/cases/1971/70-18

Sawchuk, S. (2021, May 21). What is critical race theory, and why is it under attack? *Education Week*. https://www.edweek.org/leadership/what-is-critical-race-theory-and-why-is-it-under-attack/2021/05

Singleton, G. E. (2014). *Courageous conversations about race* (2nd ed.). Corwin. Stop the Wrongs to Our Kids and Employees Act (Stop WOKE), H.B. 7 (2022). https://scholarship.law.ufl.edu/facultypub/1200/#:~:text=Florida's%20Stop%20the%20Wrongs%20to,imposes%20stiff%20sanctions%20for%20violations.

Students for Fair Admissions v. Harvard College. 600 US _ (2023). https://www.oyez.org/cases/2022/20-1199

Students for Fair Admission v. University of North Carolina. Citation pending. (2023). https://www.oyez.org/cases/2022/21-707

Sweatt v. Painter, 339 U.S. 629 (1950). https://www.oyez.org/cases/1940-1955/339us629

University of California v. Bakke, 438 US 265 (1978). https://www.oyez.org/cases/1979/76-811

Wesson, S. (2022, August 16). Education in enslaved communities. *Library of Congress Blogs*. https://blogs.loc.gov/teachers/2022/08/education-in-enslaved-communities/

CHAPTER 4

Angel, M. (2021, January). *Little evidence coffee companies' sustainability efforts have impact – report*. Reuters. https://www.reuters.com/business/little-evidence-coffee-companies-sustainability-efforts-have-impact-report-2021-01-14/

Black Lives Matter (BLM). (n.d.). https://blacklivesmatter.com

Board Diversity Action Alliance. (n.d.). https://boarddiversityactionalliance.com/

Fuhrmeister, C. (2021). Philadelphia to benefit from $100M Starbucks initiative to advance racial equity. *Philadelphia Business Journal*. https://www.bizjournals.com/philadelphia/news/2021/01/13/starbucks-racial-equity-initiative-philadelphia.html

Greenhouse, S. (2024, March). 'Huge breakthrough' in Starbucks union talks–which other US firms will follow? *The Guardian*. https://www.theguardian.com/us-news/2024/mar/22/starbucks-union-talks-trader-joes-amazon-rei

Gupta, S. (2021). Three characteristics of effective DEI leadership. *Forbes*. https://www.forbes.com/sites/forbescoachescouncil/2021/08/19/three-characteristics-of-effective-dei-leadership/?sh=43270eed10dc

Luthern, A. (2015, April 14). Dontre Hamilton family to mark one-year anniversary of shooting. *Milwaukee Journal Sentinel*. https://archive.jsonline.com/news/milwaukee/dontre-hamilton-family-to-mark-one-year-anniversary-of-shooting-b99485735z1-300847711.html

Merriam-Webster. (2023). *Kicking it with 'Kick the Can Down the Road'*. https://www.merriam-webster.com/words-at-play/kick-the-can-down-the-road-history-meaning

Morris, C. (2020, November). Performative allyship: What are the signs and why leaders get exposed. *Forbes*. https://www.forbes.com/sites/carmenmorris/2020/11/26/performative-allyship-what-are-the-signs-and-why-leaders-get-exposed/?sh=793ab5a122ec

Neuman, S. (2018). *Men arrested in Philadelphia Starbucks reach settlements*. NPR. https://www.npr.org/sections/thetwo-way/2018/05/03/607973546/men-arrested-in-philadelphia-starbucks-reach- settlements

Rethink Retail. (2020). *Starbucks avoids a gentrification reputation as it moves into underserved neighborhoods—Here's why*. https://rethink.industries/article/starbucks-avoids-a-gentrification-reputation-as-it-moves-into-underserved-neighborhoods-heres-why/

Singleton, G. E. (2022). *Courageous conversations about race: A field guide for achieving equity in schools and beyond*. Corwin.

Somaiya, R. (2015, March). Starbucks ends conversation starters on race. *The New York Times*. https://www.nytimes.com/2015/03/23/business/media/starbucks-ends-tempestuous-initiative-on-race.html

The Outline. (n.d.). *A short timeline of Starbucks' fraught history with race*. https://theoutline.com/post/4192/starbucks-racism-timeline? utm_source=trail_card

Vela, M. B., Lypson, M., & McDade, W. A. (2021). Diversity, equity, and inclusion officer position available: Proceed with caution. *Journal of Graduate Medical Education, 13*(6), 771–773.

CHAPTER 5

Aaker, J., & Chang, V. (2009). *Obama and the power of social media and technology*. Stanford Business. https://www.gsb.stanford.edu/faculty-research/case-studies/obama-power-social-media-technology

Aguilar, E. (2014). *Spheres of control*. Education Week.

Duggan, W. (2023). *A short history of the great recession*. Forbes Advisor. https://www.forbes.com/advisor/investing/great-recession/

Gottlieb, S. (2025, Winter). The clintonian roots of Obamacare. *National Affairs*, (62). https://www.nationalaffairs.com/publications/detail/the-clintonian-roots-of-obamacare

Holland, S. (2008). McCain picks Palin as vice president in U.S. election. *Reuters*. https://www.reuters.com/article/us-usa-politics-mccain-vicepresident-idUSN2940588620080829/

Kellerman, B. (2009). The nature of Obama's charismatic leadership. *Harvard Business Review*. https://hbr.org/2009/01/the-nature-of-obamas-charismat

Kosciw, J. G., Greytak, E. A., Giga, N. M., Villenas, C., & Danischewski, D. J. (2016). *The 2015 national school climate survey: The experiences of lesbian, gay, bisexual, transgender, and queer youth in our nation's schools*. GLSEN. https://www.glsen.org/sites/default/files/2020-01/GLSEN%202015%20National%20School%20Climate%20Survey%20%28NSCS%29%20-%20Full%20Report.pdf

Liptak, K. (2016). *Michelle Obama says 'angry black woman' label rooted in fear*. https://www.cnn.com/2016/12/19/politics/michelle-obama-oprah-angry-black-woman/index.html

Nasaw, D. (2008). Controversial comments made by Rev Jeremiah Wright. *The Guardian*. https://www.theguardian.com/world/2008/mar/18/barackobama.uselections20083

Poteat, V. P., & Russell, S. T. (2013). Understanding homophobic behavior and its implications for policy and practice. *Theory Into Practice*, 52(4), 264–271.

Reed, L., & Johnson, L. T. (2010). Serving LGBT students: Examining the spiritual, religious, and social justice implications for an African American school administrator. *The Journal of Negro Education*, *79*(3), 390–404.

Teaching Democracy. (2024). *Political parties platforms - election central - political parties, platforms, and planks*. https://teachdemocracy.org/election-central/political-parties-platforms.html

CHAPTER 6

Arendt, H. (2013). *The human condition*. University of Chicago Press.

Atwood, M. (1985). *The handmaid's tale*. McClelland & Stewart.

Baldwin, J. (1963). *The fire next time*. Dial Press.

Beecher, C. E. (1835). *The duty of American women to their country*. Harper & Brothers.

Beecher, C. E. (n.d.). *National women's history museum*. https://www.womenshistory.org/education-resources/biographies/catharine-esther-beecher

Bethune, M. M. (2002). *Mary McLeod Bethune: Building a better world, essays and selected* (A. T. McCluskey & E. S. Smith, eds.). Indiana University Press.

Bhagavad Gita. (Ved Vyas Foundation, Trans.) (2024). https://bhagavadgita.io/

Brown v. Board of Education, 347 U.S. 483 (1954)

Brown-Nagin, T. (2022). *Civil rights queen: Constance Baker Motley and the struggle for equality*. Vintage.

Churchill, W. (2004). *Kill the Indian, save the man: The genocidal impact of American Indian residential schools*. City Lights Publishers.

Cremin, L. A. (1980). *American education: The colonial experience, 1607-1783*. Harper & Row.

Dewey, J. (1916). *Experience and education* (N. Tampio, ed., 2024). Columbia University Press.

Elazar, D. J. (1987). *Exploring federalism*. University of Alabama Press.

Gage, B. (2018). When does a moment turn into a 'movement'? *New York Times Magazine*. https://www.nytimes.com/2018/05/15/magazine/when-does-a-moment-turn-into-a-movement.html

Gándara, P., & Contreras, F. (2009). *The Latino education crisis: The consequences of failed social policies*. Harvard University Press.

Graham, M. (2005). Booker T. Washington and the "Tuskegee Model" of education. In W. L. Andrews (Ed.), *Booker T. Washington and the African American educational experience* (pp. 53–72). University of North Carolina Press.

Hanson, J. A. (2003). *Mary McLeod Bethune and Black women's political activism* (Vol. 1). University of Missouri Press.

Height, D. (2009). *Open wide the freedom gates: A memoir*. PublicAffairs.

Holy Bible. (n.d.). *New International Version*. BibleHub. https://biblehub.com/romans/7-19.htm

Irby, D. (2021). *Stuck improving: Racial equity and school leadership*. Harvard Education Press.

Kaestle, C. F. (1983). *Pillars of the republic: Common schools and American society, 1780-1860* (Vol. 154). Macmillan.

Kobabe, M. (2019). *Gender queer: A memoir*. Oni Press.

Lee, H. (1960). *To kill a mockingbird*. J.B. Lippincott & Co.

Longshore, D. (1979). Color connotations and racial attitudes. *Journal of Black Studies*, 9(4), 183–197.

Love, B. L. (2019). *We want to do more than survive: Abolitionist teaching and the pursuit of educational freedom*. Beacon Press.

Milliken, C. (2021, Spring). How do people make change? Northwestern experts share the keys to effective social movements. *Northwestern Magazine*. https://magazine.northwestern.edu/features/how-do-people-make-change/

Qur'an, The. (M. Khattab, Trans.) (2024). https://quran.com/17?startingVerse=11.

Radin, B. A., & Boase, J. P. (2000). Federalism, political structure, and public policy in the United States and Canada. *Journal of Comparative Policy Analysis: Research and Practice*, 2(1), 65–89.

Rawls, J. (1971). *A theory of justice*. Harvard University Press eBooks. https://doi.org/10.4159/9780674042605

Reese, W. J. (2E011). *America's public schools: From the common school to "No child left behind"*. JHU Press.

Rury, J. L. (2005). *Education and social change: Contours in the history of American schooling*. Lawrence Erlbaum Associates.

Satell, G. (2016). What successful movements have in common. *Harvard Business Review*. https://hbr.org/2016/11/what-successful-movements-have-in-common

Sen, A. (2009). *The idea of justice*. Harvard University Press.

Spring, J. (2024). *American education* (21st ed.). Routledge.

Thomas, A. (2017). *The hate u give*. Balzer + Bray.

Tunnell, M. O., & Chilcoat, G. W. (2011). *The children of Topaz: The story of a Japanese-American internment camp based on a classroom diary*. Holiday House

Tyack, D. B. (1974). *The one best system* (Vol. 95). Harvard University Press.

US Department of Education. (n.d.a). *Elementary and Secondary Education Act* (ESEA) - *Overview*. https://www.ed.gov/esea

US Department of Education. (n.d.b). *Every Student Succeeds Act* (ESSA) - *Overview*. https://www.ed.gov/essa

US Department of Education. (n.d.c.) *Individuals with Disabilities Education Act* (IDEA) - *Overview*. https://sites.ed.gov/idea/

US Department of Justice. (n.d.). *Title VI of the Civil Rights Act of 1964*. https://www.justice.gov/crt/fcs/TitleVI-Overview

CHAPTER 7

Aguilar, E. (2016). Reflecting on Yourself as a Leader. *Edutopia*. https://www.edutopia.org/blog/reflecting-yourself-leader-elena-aguilar

Chen, C. W., & Gorski, P. C. (2015). Burnout in social justice and human rights activists: Symptoms, causes and implications. *Journal of Human Rights Practice*, 7(3), 366–390.

Continuous Improvement. (2024). *American society for quality*. https://asq.org/quality-resources/continuous-improvement

Geronimus, A. (2023). *The physical toll systemic injustice takes on the body*. https://time.com/6266329/systemic-injustice-health-toll-weathering/

Hernández Cárdenas, A. M., & Tello Méndez, N. G. (2017). Self-care as a political strategy. *Sur - International Journal on Human Rights*, 14, 171.

Pitts, J. (2023). *Self-care in the movement*. Learning for Social Justice. https://

www.learningforjustice.org/magazine/spring-2023/selfcare-in-the-movement

Scott, K. (2019). *Radical candor: Fully revised & updated edition: Be a kick-ass boss without losing your humanity*. St. Martin's Press.

Singleton, G. E. (2021). *Courageous conversations about race: A field guide for achieving equity in schools and beyond*. Corwin.

Smith, W. A. (2014). *Racial battle fatigue in higher education: Exposing the myth of post-racial America*. Rowman & Littlefield.

Smith, W. A., David, R., & Stanton, G. S. (2020). eRacial battle fatigue: The long-term effects of racial microaggressions on African American boys and men. In R. Majors, K. Carberry, & T. S. Ransaw (Eds.), *The international handbook of black community mental health* (pp. 83–92). Emerald Publishing Limited.

Smith, W. A., Mustaffa, J. B., Jones, C. M., Curry, T. J., & Allen, W. R. (2016). 'You make me wanna holler and throw up both my hands!': Campus culture, Black misandric microaggressions, and racial battle fatigue. *International Journal of Qualitative Studies in Education, 29*(9), 1189–1209.

Theoharis, G. (2007). Social justice educational leaders and resistance: Toward a theory of social justice leadership. *Educational Administration Quarterly, 43*(2), 221–258.

Wisconsin RtI Center (2017). *Equity: Wisconsin's Model to Inform Culturally Responsive Practices*. Wisconsin Department of Public Instruction. https://drive.google.com/file/d/1DpTjwr52XMRUPpwnwLFiGTAaAASKtQ-F/view?usp=sharing

Index

Helping educators make the greatest impact

CORWIN HAS ONE MISSION: to enhance education through intentional professional learning.

We build long-term relationships with our authors, educators, clients, and associations who partner with us to develop and continuously improve the best evidence-based practices that establish and support lifelong learning.

Zeitfracht Medien GmbH
Ferdinand-Jühlke-Straße 7
99095 Erfurt, Deutschland
produktsicherheit@kolibri360.de